Contents

Introduction

Cambridge Advanced Sciences

The *Cambridge Advanced Sciences* series has been developed to meet the demands of all the new AS and A level science examinations. In particular, it has been endorsed by OCR as providing complete coverage of their specifications. The AS material is presented as a single text for each of biology, chemistry and physics. Material for the A2 year comprises six books in each subject: one of core material and one for each option. Some material has been drawn from the existing *Cambridge Modular Sciences* books; however, many parts are entirely new.

During the development of this series, the opportunity has been taken to improve the design, and a complete and thorough new writing and editing process has been applied. Much more material is now presented in colour. Although the existing *Cambridge Modular Sciences* texts do cover most of the new specifications, the *Cambridge Advanced Sciences* books cover every OCR learning objective in detail. They are the key to success in the new AS and A level examinations.

OCR is one of the three unitary awarding bodies offering the full range of academic and vocational qualifications in the UK. For full details of the new specifications, please contact OCR:

OCR, 1 Hills Rd, Cambridge CB1 2EU
Tel: 01223 553311

The presentation of units

You will find that the books in this series use a bracketed convention in the presentation of units within tables and on graph axes. For example, ionisation energies of $1000\,\mathrm{kJ\,mol^{-1}}$ and $2000\,\mathrm{kJ\,mol^{-1}}$ will be represented in this way:

Measurement	Ionisation energy ($\mathrm{kJ\,mol^{-1}}$)
1	1000
2	2000

OCR examination papers use the solidus as a convention, thus:

Measurement	Ionisation energy / $\mathrm{kJ\,mol^{-1}}$
1	1000
2	2000

Any numbers appearing in brackets with the units, for example $(10^{-5}\,\mathrm{mol\,dm^{-3}\,s^{-1}})$, should be treated in exactly the same way as when preceded by the solidus, $/10^{-5}\,\mathrm{mol\,dm^{-3}\,s^{-1}}$.

Growth, Development and Reproduction – an A2 option text

Growth, Development and Reproduction contains everything needed to cover the A2 option of the same name. It combines entirely new text and illustrations with revised and updated material from *Growth, Development and Reproduction* previously available in the *Cambridge Modular Sciences* series. In a further improvement, the book is in full colour, greatly enhancing its accessibility and usefulness.

The book is divided into five chapters corresponding to the modules Growth and Development, Asexual Reproduction, Sexual Reproduction in Flowering Plants, Sexual Reproduction in Humans, and Control of Growth and Reproduction. All chapters have been rearranged and expanded both to aid understanding and to give more in-depth coverage of the subject.

In addition, an extensive glossary of terms is included, linked to the main text via the index.

Acknowledgements

Photographs

1.1, Phillip Colla/Ecoscene; 1.2b, 1.2d, 3.6 (left half), 3.6 (right half), 3.8, 3.12a, 3.12b, 3.15, 4.11a, 4.11b, Biophoto Associates; 1.2c, Ed Reschke, Peter Arnold Inc./Science Photo Library; 1.2e, 1.3b, John Adds; 1.11, Tommaso Guicciardini/Science Photo Library; 1.17, C Pouedras/Eurelios/Science Photo Library; 1.19, Dr Kari Lounatmaa/Science Photo Library; 2.2c CNRI/Science Photo Library; 2.2d Manfred Kage/Science Photo Library; 2.2f, Science Pictures Ltd/Science Photo Library; 2.5, Michael Holling/FLPA; 2.9, 2.10, 2.13, Nigel Cattlin/Holt Studios International; 2.12 Sinclair Stammers/Science Photo Library; 2.14 James King-Holmes/Science Photo Library; 4.8, Astrid & Hanns-Frieder Michler/Science Photo Library; 4.17, Prof P Motta/Dept of Anatomy/University 'La Sapienza', Rome/Science Photo Library; 4.19, D Phillips/Science Photo Library; 4.20, Petit Format/CSI/Science Photo Library; 4.22, Petit Format/Nestle/Science Photo Library; 4.25a, Patsy Lynch/Rex features Ltd; 4.25b, Gerry Gropp/Sipa Press; 4.27 Pascal Goetgheluck/Science Photo Library; 5.6, Mark Edwards/Still Pictures.

Picture research: Maureen Cowdroy

Diagrams and tables

Fig. 1.7 based on Silk, W K (1994) 'Kinematics and Dynamics of Primary Growth', *Biomimetics*, 2, 199–214; fig 1.9 Tanner, J M (1962) *Growth at Adolescence*, Blackwell Scientific Publications, Oxford; figs 1.14 and 1.15 after Soper, R and Smith, T (1979) *Modern Human and Social Biology*, Thomas Nelson and Sons Ltd; fig 3.17 after Green, N P O, Stout, G W, Taylor, D J & Soper, R (1990) *Biological Science*, Cambridge University Press; table 4.4 based on data from HMSO; fig 4.26 from *The Guardian*; fig. 5.1 from Hendricks, S B and Borthwick, H A (1954) 'Photoperiodism in plants' *Proceedings of the 1st International Photobiology Congress*, 23–25; fig. 5.5 from Luckwill, L C (1952) 'Growth-inhibiting and growth promoting substances in relation to the dormancy of apple seeds', reproduced by permission of *Journal of Horticultural Science*, 27, 53–67.

Growth and development

The fundamental activities of living organisms can be summarised as nutrition, growth, reproduction, respiration, excretion, sensitivity and, for some, locomotion. Two of these activities, namely growth and reproduction, are the theme of this book. Growth is usually accompanied by development, so it is usual to study both together.

What is growth?

In its usual sense, the word **growth** simply means 'getting larger'. It is something we associate with both living and non-living things. For example, crystals can grow in size, and even abstract things, like the economy, can grow.

All living things show growth and, since all living things are made of cells, growth must involve cells getting larger or increasing in number. Individual cells get larger after they have divided as they grow back to full size. Individual multicellular organisms grow in size as their cells grow in number and size. It is estimated that the average adult human contains about 50 million

cells, all of which have grown from one original cell, the zygote. The largest organism of any kind ever to have existed on this planet is the blue whale, which may grow to over 30 m in length (*figure 1.1*). This must also grow from one cell, the zygote, a programmed increase in size of

● **Figure 1.1** A blue whale, the largest living thing ever to have existed. Like all multicellular organisms produced by sexual reproduction, it has grown and developed from a single cell, the zygote.

astronomical proportions. Populations of organisms can grow in size too. The global human population reached 6000 million for the first time in 1999 and is expected to grow to at least 10 000 million before it stabilises. Starting from one cell, some bacterial populations can grow to 6000 million in just half a day given ideal conditions.

So far then, we have thought of growth as an increase in *size*. For biologists though, this definition can be improved upon. What, for example, do we mean by size? This is important to know when we want to *measure* growth. There are various measurements which could be made, as we shall see later in this chapter. Three common examples are height, length and mass. Growth of humans, for example, is often measured as increase in height. However, a person may grow in size without increasing in height simply, for example, by developing more fat, larger muscles, or a larger uterus and breasts during pregnancy. A plant may grow more leaves or shoots without growing taller. Bearing factors like this in mind, biologists consider that, overall, the most appropriate measure of growth is increase in *mass*.

SAQ 1.1
Why is growth normally associated with an increase in mass?

Biologists tend to view growth as part of a planned programme of development. Imagine a potato plant producing the potatoes that we commonly eat as vegetables. The potatoes grow underground as tubers. A tuber grows in mass as the number of its cells increases. But imagine if the soil around the tuber becomes dry. The tuber could lose water by evaporation from its surface and lose mass as a result. Then, if the soil becomes wet again, the tuber could 'grow' back to its normal mass as the cells take up water by osmosis. Would these changes in mass be signs of genuine growth? Such changes in water content are common in plant cells and can happen in any cells depending on their environment. Biologists prefer not to think of such changes as genuine growth because they are *reversible* and they are not part of programmed development. The definition of growth that most biologists prefer is that

> growth is an irreversible increase in dry mass of living material.

(Dry mass is mass after removal of water.)

SAQ 1.2
Consider the following situations and suggest why the 'growth' described might be regarded as an exception to the definition of growth given above.
a A zygote (a cell formed by the fusion of two gametes) can divide to form a ball of smaller cells with no increase in mass.
b A germinating seedling shows a net loss in dry mass (mass after removal of water) until it starts to photosynthesise. By this time much development, including that of a primary root and shoot, has taken place, accompanied by an increase in size, cell numbers and fresh mass (mass including water).

The two exceptional examples in SAQ 1.2 show that growth is a complex process for which it is difficult to give a precise definition. Although the two examples appear to contradict the definition of growth, common sense suggests that they should still be regarded as growth.

What is development?
As already mentioned, growth and development usually go hand in hand. We can say that

> development is a progressive series of changes, which includes the specialisation of cells.

In biology, development is genetically programmed and may be modified by the environment.

Multicellular organisms, such as humans or plants, grow from single cells, so growth and development must involve cell division. As each new cell is produced, it must grow to its mature size and become specialised for its essential functions. This process of specialisation is called **differentiation**. Thus growth and development typically involve three separate processes, namely:
- **cell division** leading to an increase in cell numbers;

- **cell enlargement** i.e. an increase in cell size;
- **cell differentiation** leading to cell specialisation.

SAQ 1.3 _____
What type of cell division is responsible for growth?

SAQ 1.4 _____
What is the genetic significance of mitosis?

Cell differentiation

In any multicellular organism, all the cells derived from the zygote by mitosis are genetically identical. In humans, for example, this would be all the diploid cells, that is all the cells apart from the sex cells. Therefore a liver cell, for example, contains the same set of genetic instructions as a kidney cell. The question therefore arises, how can the two cells have developed differently when they have identical DNA? It has been shown by cloning new plants and animals from differentiated cells that these cells have not lost any information as they mature. They still contain all the instructions needed to make a whole organism. We cannot say therefore that a liver cell has lost the DNA needed to become a kidney cell. Instead, as cells differentiate, different genes are 'switched' 'on' or 'off'. In a liver cell the 'liver genes' are switched on and other genes are switched off; in a kidney cell the 'kidney genes' are switched on and other genes are switched off. The study of how this differing 'behaviour' of cells is controlled may lead to new techniques for treating a variety of medical disorders using **stem cells**. These are undifferentiated cells, found in e.g. young embryos, able to develop into any of the organism's cell types.

At any one time, a particular cell will have a variety of genes switched on or off in response to its environment without losing its identifying characteristics. For example, a fully mature pancreas cell is still a pancreas cell whether or not it is secreting insulin.

Growth and development in plants

The location of growth and development within an organism differs between animals and plants. In animals, cell division can occur throughout the body. In complex animals the body develops systems made up of organs, and all these organs contain cells capable of dividing. In plants, however, cell division is much more localised. In fact, it can only occur in particular regions called meristems (from the Greek *merizein*, to divide). Growth in *length* occurs from **apical meristems**, found at the tips of roots and shoots ('apical' comes from 'apex', meaning tip). Growth in *width* occurs from **lateral meristems**, which are found along the length of roots and shoots.

> A meristem is a region of unspecialised plant cells from which new cells arise by cell division.

When a meristem cell divides, one of the cells produced remains **meristematic**. The other cell gives rise to one or more specialised cells. All the cells, tissues and organs of a plant are derived from meristems.

The three stages of growth mentioned previously, namely cell division, cell enlargement and cell differentiation, are all shown particularly clearly in the apical regions of roots and shoots because they are separated in time and place. (This will be explained below.) In animals, these three phases of growth also occur, but it is usually much harder to locate the exact position of the growing cells and to follow the sequence of events clearly. It is therefore useful to study plant root tips and shoot tips as 'models' of growth.

Root tips

Root tips are responsible for the increase in length of the roots. *Figure 1.2a* is a diagram of a longitudinal section (LS) through a root tip and shows three **zones**. Moving back from the tip, these are the zones of cell division, then cell enlargement and then cell differentiation. This is a time sequence, with the youngest cells being the dividing cells near the tip and the most mature being the differentiated cells furthest away from the tip. *Figure 1.2b* shows a photograph of a section through a root tip. The **zone of cell division** in the root tip (*figure 1.2c*) keeps producing new cells while the root is growing. In the **zone of cell enlargement**, the new cells get larger by taking up water by osmosis and synthesising new

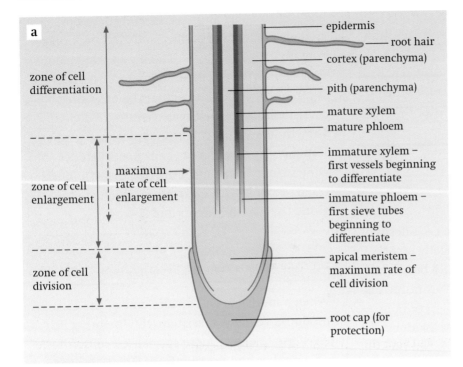

a

zone of cell differentiation

zone of cell enlargement

maximum rate of cell enlargement

zone of cell division

epidermis

root hair

cortex (parenchyma)

pith (parenchyma)

mature xylem

mature phloem

immature xylem – first vessels beginning to differentiate

immature phloem – first sieve tubes beginning to differentiate

apical meristem – maximum rate of cell division

root cap (for protection)

● **Figure 1.2**
a Simplified diagram of LS of a root tip.
b Photomicrograph of LS root tip of *Vicia faba* (broad bean) (× 100).
c Cells from zone of cell division (× 250).
d Cells from zone of cell enlargement (× 1500).
e Cells from zone of cell differentiation.

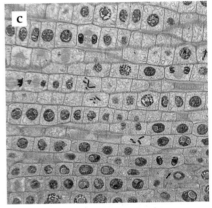

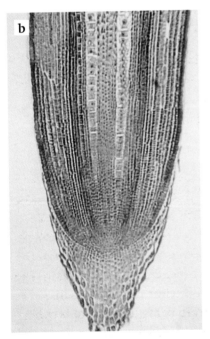

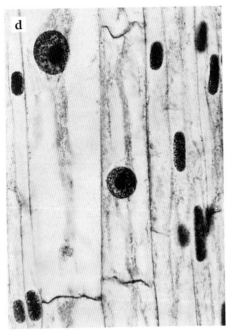

materials, often becoming much longer (*figure 1.2d*). In the **zone of cell differentiation**, the cells become specialised for particular functions and develop specialised structures. Three examples are:

■ **xylem**, made from cells called xylem vessel elements which fuse together as they differentiate to form long, dead tubes specialised for transporting water and mineral salts over long distances (*figure 1.2e* and *Biology 1*, chapter 10);

■ **phloem**, containing long, living tubes called sieve tubes, again made by cells (called sieve tube elements) fusing together. Sieve tubes are specialised to transport organic solutes such as sucrose around the plant (*Biology 1*, chapter 10);

■ **epidermis**, the outermost layer. Epidermal cells have a protective function. In roots they may grow extensions, the root hairs, to increase the surface area for water absorption.

Remember that all these cells contain identical DNA and therefore identical sets of genes. The control of differentiation involves the switching on and off of different genes in different cells at

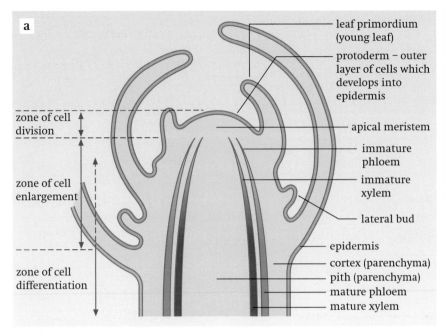

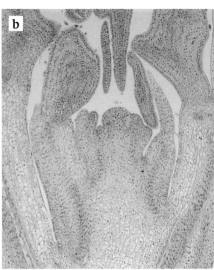

labels (figure a):
leaf primordium (young leaf)
protoderm – outer layer of cells which develops into epidermis
apical meristem
immature phloem
immature xylem
lateral bud
epidermis
cortex (parenchyma)
pith (parenchyma)
mature phloem
mature xylem

zone of cell division
zone of cell enlargement
zone of cell differentiation

● **Figure 1.3 a** Simplified diagram of LS of a shoot tip. **b** Photo of LS of a shoot tip.

different times. Cells that become xylem vessel elements, for example, must synthesise the strengthening material lignin, which reinforces their walls. They must therefore have enzymes that control the synthesis of lignin. The genes that control production of these enzymes must therefore be switched on in cells that become xylem vessel elements.

We can now summarise how the root tip provides a good example of growth and development. Growth involves an irreversible increase in size and this is brought about by cell division in the apical meristem followed by cell enlargement. The process is irreversible because new materials and structures are added. Examples of these are proteins, such as enzymes, and entire new organelles inside the cells, and lignin in the cell walls of xylem vessel elements. We know that development is a progressive series of changes that includes the specialisation of cells. This is shown clearly here by the changes that cells undergo, from small meristematic cells in the zone of cell division to the range of cells seen in the zone of differentiation. We also saw earlier that development is genetically programmed and may be modified by the environment. This is also shown by the root. The root has evolved to respond to certain environmental stimuli such as gravity, moisture and light. Roots usually grow downwards in response to gravity, and towards water. They tend

to grow away from light. These are just a few of the many ways in which environment helps to determine the development of organs such as roots. The root tip thus illustrates general principles of growth and development which apply to *all* multicellular organisms.

Shoot tips

The shoot tip is a more complex structure than the root tip because it also grows leaves and buds. Each leaf starts growth as a small swelling called a leaf primordium. As well as this, a bud develops between the leaf and the stem, known as a lateral bud or axillary bud depending on its position. The bud has the potential to form a new branch.

Despite the shoot tip being more complex than the root tip, their growth shows the same principles. Zones of cell division, cell enlargement and cell differentiation can be recognised, as shown in *figure 1.3*. This is particularly well illustrated by the development of the vascular tissue (the xylem and phloem).

Types of growth curve

Before we look in detail at ways of measuring growth, we shall consider how best to describe growth and show it in the form of graphs. Graphs showing growth are known as **growth curves**.

Growth is usually recorded in one of three ways:

- absolute growth;
- absolute growth rate;
- relative growth rate.

For each of these a growth curve can be constructed.

Absolute growth curves

Absolute growth is increase in size or mass with time. Absolute growth is also known as actual growth. A graph which shows absolute growth has time on the *x* axis and size on the *y* axis, and is called an absolute growth curve. It is the simplest way of showing growth.

Absolute growth curves are useful for showing:

- the overall pattern of growth;
- how much growth has taken place.

The sigmoid curve

Absolute growth curves often have a simple mathematical form such as a straight line or, more commonly, a sigmoid shape (S-shape) (*figure 1.4a*). Some common examples of sigmoid-shaped growth are:

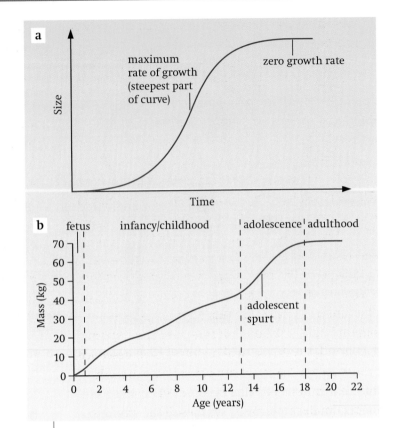

● **Figure 1.4** Absolute growth curves.
a Idealised S-shaped (sigmoid) absolute growth curve.
b Absolute growth curve for a sample of humans. Growth is measured as increase in mass. Four phases of growth are shown.

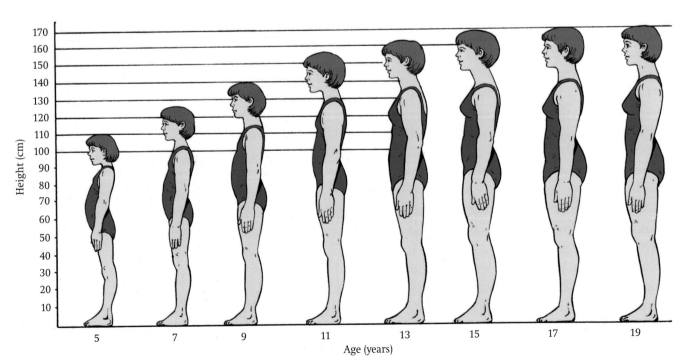

● **Figure 1.5** The growth in height of an average human female from age 5 to 19 years. Note: there is a great deal of variation between individuals.

- many multicellular organisms, e.g. annual plants, insects, birds, mammals (including humans);
- some parts of organisms, e.g. leaves and fruits;
- the population growth of microorganisms and many other natural populations.

Figure 1.4a shows an idealised sigmoid growth curve. Growth is slow at first but, as the size of the organism or population increases, the rate of growth increases and this forms the steep part of the graph. The larger the organism or population, the faster it grows, until a maximum growth rate is reached. Then growth slows down until it stops and the graph levels off, completing the S shape. At this point the maximum size has been reached.

Figure 1.4b shows the increase in mass with age of a sample of humans. This approximates to a sigmoid curve, although it is complicated by small spurts of growth, particularly during adolescence. *Figures 1.5* and *1.6* show respectively the growth and development of a human female and a human male from age 5–19 years. The absolute growth curves could be drawn by drawing a line from head to head in the equally spaced diagrams.

SAQ 1.5

The positions of two cells in the growing root of a maize plant were noted at different times. The positions were measured as distance from the end of the root tip. The results are shown in *figure 1.7*. The zone of cell division occupied the bottom 2 mm of the root tip. The zone of cell enlargement extended from 2–10 mm from the end of the tip.

a How far was cell 1 from cell 2 at the start of the experiment?

b How far was cell 1 from cell 2 after 5 hours?

c Explain the difference between your answers to a and b.

d How far back from the end of the root tip would you first expect to find mature xylem?

e Explain why the distance from the end of the root tip of both cells 1 and 2 increases with time.

f Explain why the distance of cell 2 from the end of the root tip increases most rapidly after about 7 hours.

g If the root continues to grow at the same rate, what shape would the curves show between 20 and 40 hours?

h At what rate is the root growing through the soil?

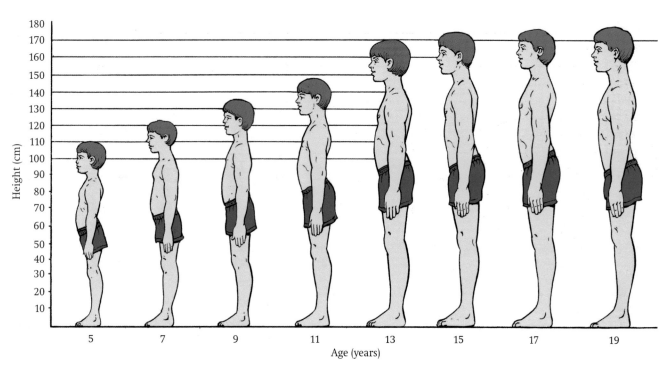

● **Figure 1.6** The growth in height of an average human male from age 5 to 19 years.
Note: there is a great deal of variation between individuals.

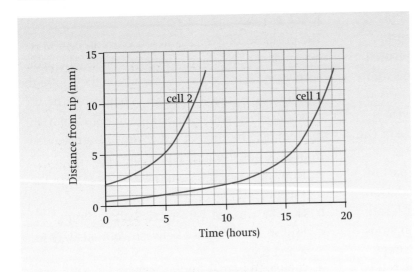

● **Figure 1.7** Changes in the distance of two cells from the end of a growing maize root tip.

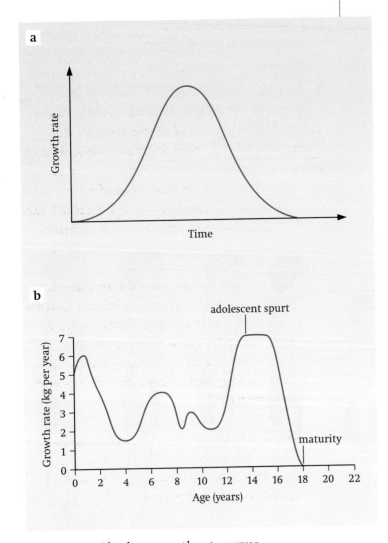

● **Figure 1.8** Absolute growth rate curves.
a Absolute growth rate curve derived from the sigmoid curve shown in *figure 1.4a*.
b Absolute growth rate curve for a sample of humans measured as rate of increase of mass against time (age).

Absolute growth rate curves

Absolute growth rate is the absolute growth in a given time period, e.g. an increase in height of 4 cm per year. An absolute growth rate curve has time on the *x* axis and growth rate on the *y* axis.

Absolute growth rate curves are useful for showing:

■ when growth is most rapid (the peak of the curve);
■ how the rate of growth changes with time (the slope of the curve).

The bell-shaped curve

When a sigmoid curve showing absolute growth is converted to an absolute growth *rate* curve it shows a typical 'bell' shape, as in *figure 1.8a*. The peak of the bell shape represents the highest rate of growth. This corresponds to the steepest part of the sigmoid curve in *figure 1.4a*. The final growth rate in the bell-shaped curve is zero. This corresponds to the plateau at the top of the sigmoid curve in *figure 1.4a*.

Figure 1.8b is an absolute growth rate curve of a sample of humans, measured as increase in mass per year at different ages. Note that a fall in the graph indicates a slowing of growth, not a loss of mass. Note also that a horizontal line does not mean that growth has stopped, but that the rate of growth is constant (see adolescent spurt). At maturity the absolute growth rate is zero.

SAQ 1.6

Figure 1.9 shows absolute growth rate curves for boys and girls based on height.
a Describe the difference in growth between boys and girls as shown by the curves.
b Which sex is taller on average at the beginning of the adolescent spurt? Explain your answer.
c At what age is the maximum growth rate for (i) girls and (ii) boys in the sample?
d What is the growth rate for (i) girls and (ii) boys at the peak of the adolescent spurt?

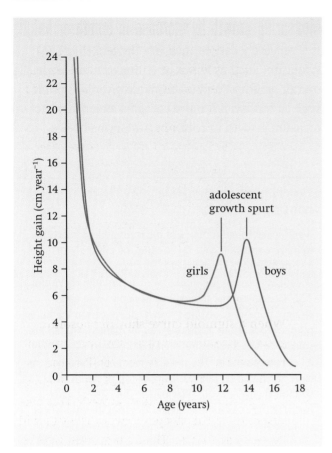

● **Figure 1.9** Absolute growth rate curve for boys and girls based on height.

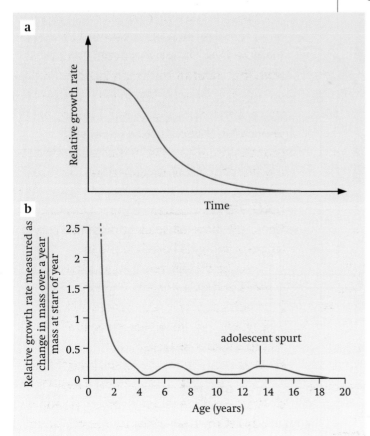

Relative growth rate curves

If a boy of two years old and one of 14 years old are both growing at a rate of 10 cm per year their absolute growth rates are the same. However, if the sizes of the two boys are taken into account, the two-year-old boy is growing relatively faster because 10 cm is a greater *relative* increase in height for him. The relative sizes of individuals can be taken into account by calculating the **relative growth rate**.

The relative growth rate for height can be calculated as:

$$\frac{\text{change in height in one year}}{\text{height at beginning of year}}$$

or

$$\frac{\text{absolute growth rate}}{\text{height at beginning of year}}$$

So a relative growth rate curve has time on the *x* axis and relative growth rate on the *y* axis. (Other measures of growth, such as mass, can be used instead of height.) Relative growth rate curves are useful for showing how efficiently an organism is growing at different ages. A high relative growth rate indicates a high efficiency of growth, because the growth rate is high relative to the size of the organism.

Shape of curve

When a bell-shaped curve showing absolute growth rate is converted to a relative growth rate curve, the shape is as shown in *figure 1.10a*. A relative growth rate curve for a sample of humans is shown in *figure 1.10b*. Note the very high relative growth rate early in human life.

SAQ 1.7

From what you have studied so far in this chapter, suggest at least three ways in which growth could be measured.

● **Figure 1.10**
a Relative growth rate curve derived from *figure 1.8a*.
b Relative growth rate curve for a sample of humans.

Measuring growth in plants

Having looked at growth curves, we will now consider the various ways in which growth can be measured. Being able to measure and analyse growth has a number of important applications. For example, the growth of crops and domestic livestock such as cattle is of obvious commercial significance if not a matter of survival. If techniques are available for measuring growth, the effects of important variables such as light, water, mineral availability, sowing density for crops, and diet and shelter for livestock, can be investigated. Optimum (ideal) growth conditions can then be found. With plants, experiments are commonly carried out in special growth rooms in which environmental variables can be controlled and one variable at a time investigated (figure 1.11).

Growth in plants is most commonly measured by increase in height, length, dry mass, or fresh mass. Each method has its advantages and disadvantages, but let us first look at the techniques themselves.

● **Figure 1.11** A typical growth room.

Measuring growth by increase in length or height

It is relatively easy to measure the length of structures such as leaves or fruits, or to measure the overall height of a plant from a convenient point such as soil level. A more complex experiment to measure growth of root tips is described below.

Experiment to measure growth in length of root tips

A well-established method of measuring plant growth is to mark a growing root tip at equal intervals, about 1–2 mm apart, with Indian ink and then measure the distances between the marks at 24-hour intervals (figure 1.12). Peas or runner beans have suitably large and straight primary roots (first roots). Starting from the tip, a primary root about 2 cm long can be marked with an ink-soaked cotton thread stretched taut between the ends of a bent piece of wire. The peas, runner beans or other large seeds can be pinned near the top of pieces of softboard covered with filter paper. The base of each board is then placed in a beaker of water and the whole covered with polythene. Overall changes in length, and percentage increases in length, for each interval marked on the primary root can be plotted on graphs. The various types of growth curve already discussed on pages 8–9 can then be plotted.

Since dividing cells are found only in the root tip, enlarging cells just behind the tip and differentiating cells still further from the tip, the marks in the enlargement zone move further apart and those in the differentiation zone stay approximately the same distance apart (figure 1.12).

Note that a full definition of growth should include both cell division and cell differentiation as well as cell enlargement, and this technique only measures cell enlargement. More elaborate techniques involving microscopy are used to measure the numbers of cells and their degree of differentiation.

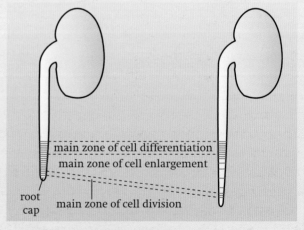

● **Figure 1.12** Growth in a root tip.

SAQ 1.8

Table 1.1 provides data on the growth of oat plants from seed.
a Draw a graph of height against time.
b What type of growth curve have you drawn?
c What other types of growth curve could be obtained from the data?

Time from sowing (days)	Mean height (cm)
0	0
2	0
4	1.5
6	5.0
8	10.8
10	19.3
14	28.8
21	43.2
28	55.2
35	62.6
42	74.8
49	89.3
56	96.7

● **Table 1.1** Growth in height of oat plants from seed.

Time from sowing (days)	Mean total dry mass (mg)	Mean dry mass of endosperm (mg)	Mean dry mass of embryo (mg)
0	43	41	2
2	41	39	2
4	38	30	8
6	34	18	16
8	33	9	24
10	34	4	30
14	38		
21	50		
28	108		
35	201		
42	432		
49	865		
56	1707		
63	2765		

● **Table 1.2** Changes in dry mass of oat plants during germination and early growth.

Measuring growth by increase in mass

It is more difficult and time-consuming to measure changes in mass than changes in length or height but there are advantages (see later) and the method is as follows.

In order to standardise conditions when carrying out experiments, (see later) large numbers of seeds of the chosen plant, for example pea or wheat, can be germinated in a commercial compost or in a sterile non-soil medium such as vermiculite, and watered with a standard culture solution containing the required mineral salts. Fresh mass (that is, including water content) can be measured after blotting dry a sample of the plants to remove excess liquid. (Various other measurements may also be recorded at the same time, such as leaf length, the distance between leaves (internode) and root length, plant height, and number or area of leaves.) Dry mass can subsequently be determined by drying in a warm area for 24 hours, weighing, and repeating the procedure every 24 hours until the mass is constant.

Efforts must be made to make the samples truly representative, which ideally means taking the mean value of at least 30 individual plants and ensuring that, as far as possible, all plants grow under identical conditions. A suitable procedure might be as follows.

Start with 300 seeds, and soak them in water for 24 hours. Take a sample of 30 for fresh and dry mass determinations and plant the remainder. Further samples of 30 can then be taken at, for example, two-day intervals. When the seedling stage is reached the masses of whole seedlings, including roots, should be determined. Graphs of mean mass against time can be plotted for the first 20 days of growth.

SAQ 1.9

Table 1.2 provides further data on the growth of the same oat plants as *table 1.1*. (The **endosperm** is the food store in cereal seeds and the **embryo** grows into the new oat plant.)
a Draw absolute growth curves to show changes in total dry mass, dry mass of endosperm and dry mass of embryo over the first 10 days from sowing. Draw the three graphs on the same pair of axes so that they can be compared easily.
b Describe and try to account for the changes in (i) dry mass of the endosperm and (ii) dry mass of the embryo over the first 10 days after sowing and (iii) total dry mass over the first eight days after sowing.
c Draw a further graph on another set of axes to show the changes in total dry mass over the first 63 days (nine weeks) after sowing.
d Describe and suggest reasons for the changes in total dry mass between eight days and 63 days after sowing.

SAQ 1.10

Figure 1.13 shows changes in dry mass and rate of growth of a plant over a period of 40 days from the start of germination. Rate of growth was calculated by measuring the change in dry mass per day.

a Which graph, A or B, represents dry mass and which graph represents rate of growth?

b State one important way in which you would expect a graph showing increase in shoot length to differ from graph B.

c What types of growth curve are A and B?

d Describe the shape of graph B.

e Why is there a negative growth rate immediately after germination?

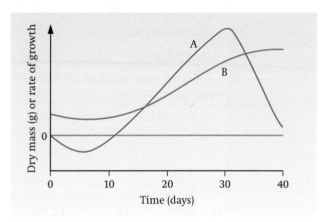

● **Figure 1.13** Growth of a plant.

Measuring growth in animals

Measuring the growth of animals presents a new set of problems compared with plants. Much of our detailed knowledge has come from humans or from farm and laboratory animals because trapping wild animals and taking measurements from them is difficult. Insects, however, are useful animals for growth studies as they are convenient to keep and grow relatively quickly. They also show an interesting split into two groups with very different growth characteristics.

Insect life cycles and growth

Insects belong to a large and successful group of animals known as the arthropods, which also includes crustaceans, centipedes, millipedes, scorpions and spiders. One of the distinguishing features of the arthropods, and one reason for their success as a group, is that they all possess an **exoskeleton** ('exo' means 'outside'). This is a tough, fairly rigid layer which covers the body and is secreted by the epidermis. It functions as a skeleton because it provides support and muscles are attached to it. It can be thin and light, as in insects, or thick and hard for protection, as in crabs. It also has a waterproof layer to help prevent desiccation (drying out).

Having an exoskeleton imposes some limitations on arthropods, however. For example, the exoskeleton cannot grow in size. Arthropods therefore grow by shedding their exoskeletons at regular intervals, a process known as **ecdysis** (the Greek word for 'moulting'). A new, soft exoskeleton is grown before the old one is shed. After moulting, this stretches, partly due to the pressure of new growth that has already occurred since the last moult, and partly due to the uptake of water or air by the animal. The volume occupied by this water or air can be replaced with new tissue after the new exoskeleton has hardened until, in its turn, the new exoskeleton becomes too small. The period between each moult is known as an **instar** (a Latin word meaning 'form'). Growth therefore appears to take place in a series of steps, with a sudden increase in size at each step. In insects, the number of instars is usually pre-determined and the adult does not moult any further.

Metamorphosis

Before considering the effect of regular moulting on growth curves, it is important to recognise that most insects also undergo metamorphosis during growth. **Metamorphosis** is a change in form from a larval stage to an adult stage during the life cycle. It is also characteristic of amphibians, as in the change from tadpole (larva) to frog (adult). Insects show two types of metamorphosis, known as complete and incomplete metamorphosis (*figure 1.14*).

■ **Complete metamorphosis.** A total change in form takes place with the result that the adult is physically very different from the larva and so usually has a completely different way of life and food source. For example, the adult mosquito flies but its larva is aquatic. Good examples of insects with complete metamorphosis are butterflies and moths, where the

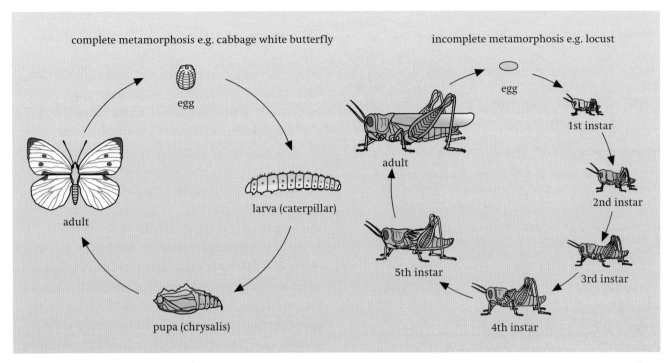

complete metamorphosis e.g. cabbage white butterfly

egg

adult

larva (caterpillar)

pupa (chrysalis)

incomplete metamorphosis e.g. locust

egg

1st instar

2nd instar

3rd instar

4th instar

5th instar

adult

● **Figure 1.14** The two types of life cycle in insects, complete and incomplete metamorphosis.

larva is a caterpillar, and flies, where the larva is a maggot. Other examples are beetles, bees, wasps, ants and fleas. There are four stages in the life cycle:

1 **egg**
2 **larva** – undergoes a series of moults as it grows. Wings develop internally but are not visible.
3 **pupa** – the body of the larva is broken down and reorganised into the adult form.
4 **adult (imago)** – winged.

■ **Incomplete metamorphosis.** A gradual change in form takes place from larva to adult and there is no pupa stage. The larva is often referred to as a **nymph** (or **naiad** if aquatic). As with complete metamorphosis, the larva undergoes a series of moults as it grows. Each successive stage is larger and more like the adult, though only the adult has functional wings. Examples of insects with incomplete metamorphosis are locusts, grasshoppers, cockroaches, dragonflies, mayflies, stoneflies, aphids, earwigs and bugs. The nymphs of locusts and grasshoppers are sometimes called 'hoppers' because they cannot fly.

Measuring growth of insects

If you were trying to measure the growth of an insect showing incomplete metamorphosis, such as locust or grasshopper, an obvious method might be to measure body length at regular intervals. However, growth curves based on length have an unusual appearance (*figure 1.15*) because growth appears to take place in a series of spurts, with no growth in-between. This is very misleading, because a growth curve based on the increase in dry mass of the insect is a smoother, typically S-shaped, or sigmoid curve (as in *figure 1.4a*). Such growth starts rapidly then begins to slow down and finally ceases. Thus the *true* growth of the insect, based on irreversible increase in dry mass, is continuous and does not have the interrupted pattern shown in *figure 1.15*. The reason for the stepped growth curve for changes in body length is that the exoskeleton is too rigid to allow expansion. Growth in length is therefore confined to brief periods after moulting of the old exoskeleton, when a new exoskeleton is forming and is still flexible.

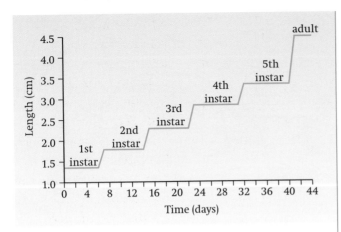

● **Figure 1.15** Growth curve based on body length for the short-horned grasshopper.

SAQ 1.11

Suggest two ways in which the daily growth of an insect could be measured, other than by determining increase in body length or dry mass.

SAQ 1.12

A representative sample of locust instars and adults was collected and the lengths of the head, tibia (part of the hind leg) and wings were accurately measured. Mean lengths revealed the following features of growth and development:

■ head – maximum rate of growth early in development;

■ tibia – steady rate of growth throughout development;

■ wings – maximum rate of growth late in development.

How might the changes observed be related to the life cycle of the insect?

Measuring growth in microorganisms and populations

Growth can be studied at any level of biological organisation, from cells, organs and organisms to populations and communities. You may remember from *Biology 1*, chapter 7 that a **population** is a group of organisms of the same species living together in a given place at a given time that can interbreed with each other. The term could refer, for example, to all the badgers living in an oak wood, or to all the bacteria living in a test-tube. Studying the growth of populations is important for a number of reasons. In agriculture, for instance, it is useful to know about the growth of pest populations. This might allow the more effective timing of spraying with pesticides. The growth of human populations is another major concern. If we are to control human population growth, for example, we need to understand what factors are important in regulating the growth.

Very simple single-celled organisms such as yeasts and bacteria are a useful starting point when we wish to study population growth. Because large numbers can be grown relatively quickly, they can be used to model population growth under ideal conditions, and to investigate some of the factors which can limit population growth. In a typical experiment, a small number of such microorganisms are introduced (inoculated) into a suitable nutrient medium and their population size monitored over a period of time. The nutrient media used will generally allow the growth of a wide range of microorganisms, so contamination must be prevented. It is therefore usual to use aseptic techniques, which involve using sterilised apparatus and materials.

It is outside the scope of this book to describe in detail how to carry out experiments using aseptic techniques. The techniques are highly specialised and must be conducted with regard to the possible health hazards involved in handling bacteria. Reference should therefore be made to more specialised books, such as *Microbiology and Biotechnology* in this series, if practical work is to be carried out. In this chapter we shall look at some of the principles involved in measuring growth of populations of unicellular microorganisms. Outline descriptions of some procedures used and some of the problems commonly encountered also follow.

In order to measure population growth, the number of individuals in representative samples has to be counted at regular intervals. Two types of count may be used, namely **viable counts**, which include living cells only, and **total counts**, which include all cells, living plus dead.

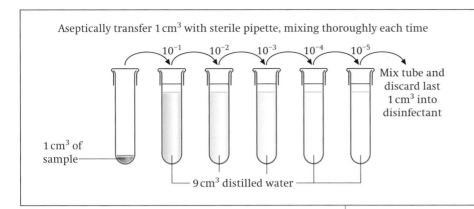

Aseptically transfer 1 cm³ with sterile pipette, mixing thoroughly each time

10^{-1} 10^{-2} 10^{-3} 10^{-4} 10^{-5}

Mix tube and discard last 1 cm³ into disinfectant

1 cm³ of sample

9 cm³ distilled water

● **Figure 1.16** Making a serial dilution.

Serial dilution

In practice, a sample may contain too many cells to count easily using the techniques described below. In this situation it is usual to prepare a series of dilutions of the sample so that one of the dilutions will prove to have a suitable concentration of cells. A correction factor can then be applied to allow for the dilution once the count has been made. A common technique for serial dilution is as follows. (Remember, all procedures must be carried out under aseptic conditions.)

1 cm³ of the culture in a liquid medium is taken in a sterile pipette and mixed thoroughly with 9 cm³ of sterile distilled water, making a total of 10 cm³. This dilutes the original by 10 times, a 10^{-1} dilution. A 1 cm³ sample of the 10^{-1} dilution is then added to 9 cm³ sterile distilled water as before to produce a 10^{-2} dilution. This procedure can be repeated to produce a dilution series down to an appropriate concentration such as 10^{-6} or 10^{-12} (*figure 1.16*).

Viable counts

Viable counts are used when it is important to know the number of *living* microorganisms. For example, the effect of pasteurising milk could be investigated by finding the total number of living bacteria in samples of milk taken before and after pasteurisation. The most common method of viable counting of bacteria is based on the basic principle that, given a suitable medium in which to grow, each bacterium in a sample will multiply over one or two days to produce one visible colony.

A typical procedure is as follows:

1 Add a known small volume (for example, 0.1 cm³) of each sample to molten nutrient agar jelly in a separate petri dish. Setting up two or more identical cultures (**replication**) for each sample and averaging the results ensures more accurate results and gives an indication of how much variation can occur merely as a result of the technique.

2 Rotate to mix, and allow the agar to set.

3 Set up a **control** nutrient agar dish with no bacteria. No bacteria should grow in this. This is a check that the technique is not allowing contamination by other bacteria.

4 Incubate the cultures as appropriate for the particular organism, for example at 30 °C for 24 hours. Then count the number of colonies in each dish. In theory, this should equal the number of bacteria in the original sample added to the dish (*figure 1.17*).

5 In some instances there are so many colonies in the petri dish or tube that it is impossible to count them. In such cases, a dilution series should be prepared as described in the previous section.

Another method of viable counting is to measure a product of metabolism such as a gas (for example, carbon dioxide from

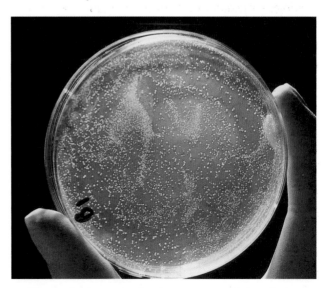

● **Figure 1.17** Colonies in an agar dish.

respiration) or an acid. Such a method could be used for yeasts as well as bacteria.

There are several problems associated with viable counting.

■ Aseptic (sterile) procedures require special apparatus and techniques. Contamination occurs easily.

■ If more than one type of bacterium is present in a sample, as in milk, the culture conditions will not favour them all equally.

■ Bacteria are rarely distributed evenly throughout a sample. They are often found in clumps of variable numbers, so a single colony could be derived from many bacteria. It is therefore difficult to obtain reproducible results. However, high levels of accuracy are not often needed because the numbers are so large.

■ Some bacteria are pathogenic (cause disease). Care is therefore required with handling, and there are restrictions on the bacteria that can be grown in schools or colleges.

Total counts

Unlike viable counts, which measure only living microorganisms, total counts measure both living *and* dead cells in the sample. A number of methods may be used to obtain total counts. They can be used for bacteria and yeasts. **Direct counting** of the number of cells in a known volume is possible using a microscope and a special slide known as a **haemocytometer slide** (*figure 1.18a*). It is designed so that a known volume of sample covers a ruled grid. A representative sample of cells can thus be counted and estimates can be made of the number in the total sample. Again, it is useful to prepare a dilution series. The central section of the slide is thinner than the rest of the slide so that when a coverslip is placed over this section, a space, usually 0.1 mm deep, is left below it (*figure 1.18b*). When the coverslip is in place, a small volume of the sample is added under the coverslip by holding a pipette against the side of the coverslip. This fills the space with an exact volume of liquid. The number of cells in a representative sample of grid squares is counted, and using the dilution factor the number in the original sample is calculated. At least 600 cells should be counted. Where cells overlap the grid lines they are usually judged as in the

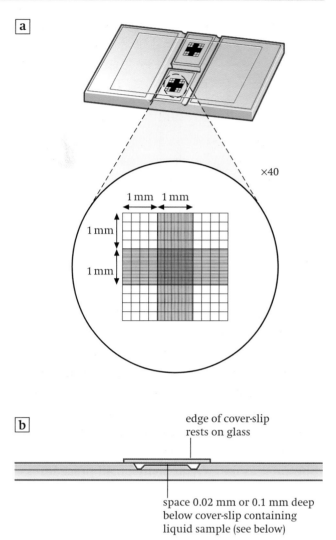

Figure 1.18 Haemocytometer slide.

square on two sides, e.g. top and left, and out of the square on the other two sides, rather than trying to count parts of cells, or risk counting the same cell twice. (Also see page 31, *Microbiology and Biotechnology* in this series.)

In the case of yeasts, the use of a stain which only stains dead cells, such as methylene blue, may allow a viable count to be made. Direct counting has several disadvantages.

■ The technique requires practice.

■ The slide must be scrupulously clean.

■ It is difficult to distinguish bacteria from other small particulate matter.

■ Bacteria are often not evenly distributed throughout a sample, so small samples may result in large errors.

Another common method for obtaining a total count depends on the fact that the more bacteria there are in a solution, the more turbid (cloudy) it appears. **Turbidity methods** measure the amount of light that is transmitted through a suspension of the bacteria using a colorimeter. If necessary, *actual* numbers can be obtained by comparing the turbidity of unknown samples with the turbidity of samples containing known numbers.

Bacterial population growth curve

The growth curve of a population of bacteria was examined in detail in *Biology 2*, pages 49–50. You may remember that the curve could be divided into the following phases: **lag phase**, **log phase** (exponential phase), **stationary phase** and **decline phase** (death phase).

It was also shown that the growth curve is sigmoid up to the beginning of the decline phase (*figure 1.19*). Note that the vertical axis in *figure 1.19* is logarithmic, so the exponential phase of growth appears as a straight line if the theoretical maximum rate of growth is achieved.

SAQ 1.13
Starting with one bacterium, how many bacteria would be present after five hours assuming exponential growth and the ability of the bacteria to grow and divide every 30 minutes?

SAQ 1.14
Why does a lag phase often precede the log phase?

SAQ 1.15
State three factors which could cause the growth rate to start to decline.

SAQ 1.16
At which stage does **a** the rate of dying equal the rate of production of new cells, **b** the rate of dying exceed the rate of production of new cells?

We can learn some important principles from laboratory studies of microorganisms. However, understanding the population growth of organisms under *natural* conditions is often far more difficult. This is because many more factors are important variables. Such factors include

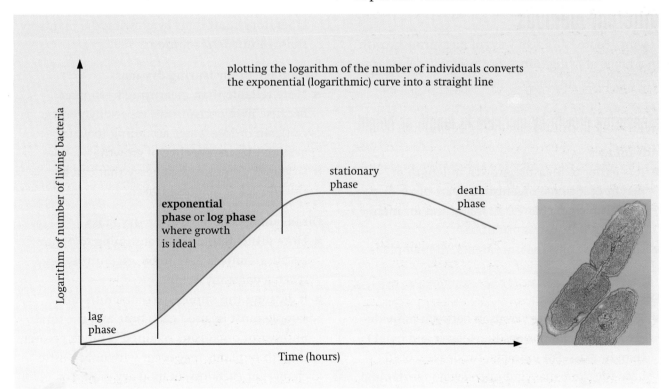

plotting the logarithm of the number of individuals converts the exponential (logarithmic) curve into a straight line

Logarithm of number of living bacteria

exponential phase or **log phase** where growth is ideal

stationary phase

death phase

lag phase

Time (hours)

● **Figure 1.19** Typical growth curve of a bacterial population. The vertical axis is logarithmic. The photograph is a transmission electron micrograph of *Salmonella typhimurium* dividing (× 20 200).

competition (between species as well as within a species), disease, climate, predation, population density and parasitism. Their study is part of a branch of biology known as population ecology (*Biology 2*, chapter 3), but other areas of biology, such as animal behaviour, are also relevant. Observations of natural populations suggest that under a given set of environmental conditions, natural population sizes tend to stabilise and stay reasonably constant over long periods of time. In other words, they show typically sigmoid growth curves and do not enter a phase of decline. Each population comes into a dynamic equilibrium with its environment. This was first pointed out by the clergyman and mathematician Thomas Malthus at the end of the eighteenth century and was one of the observations which formed the basis of Darwin's theory of natural selection. Humans are an interesting example of an animal species which is not at present in equilibrium with its environment, and how we achieve such an equilibrium presents us with one of our greatest challenges as a species.

Advantages and disadvantages of different methods

Having studied different ways of measuring growth in a range of living things, it is useful to summarise some of their advantages and disadvantages.

Measuring growth by increase in length or height

Advantages
- It is easier to measure growth in length or height of a whole organism or part of an organism than changes in mass, and for many purposes it is just as useful.
- Unlike dry mass measurements, the sample is not destroyed.

Disadvantages
- There may be more variation between individuals in linear dimensions like length and height than in mass. For example, two leaves could have the same mass but one may be shorter and wider. Measuring length would give a misleading interpretation of growth. Mass is therefore

more representative of true growth than length in this case.
- Shoots may grow in length but not irreversibly increase mass. For example if growing in the dark, a shoot cannot add new dry mass by photosynthesis. It also continues to lose dry mass in the form of CO_2 during respiration. Similarly, roots may elongate during germination with no increase in mass.

Measuring growth by increase in mass

Advantages
The measurement of mass is generally regarded as a better guide to growth than the measurement of single dimensions such as height or length because:
- it is more representative of the whole organism or structure;
- it is a better guide to the eventual yield in agriculture.

Mass may be measured as fresh mass or dry mass.

Advantage of measuring fresh mass
- Easier than measuring dry mass. Usually, relatively easy to weigh the whole organism. The problem of removing soil from the roots of plants before weighing can be avoided under laboratory conditions by growing the plants in soil-free nutrient solutions.

Advantage of measuring dry mass
- More reliable than measuring fresh mass because living organisms, especially plants, can gain or lose water according to water availability, irrespective of growth.
- Dry mass contains the energy that can be traced back to photosynthesis.

Disadvantages of measuring dry mass
- More difficult and time-consuming to obtain because samples have to be dried until they reach a constant weight.
- It destroys the sample, so that a different sample must be used each time and the total number of organisms required is much greater.
- Growth in plants may occur with only a little change, or even loss, in total dry mass. For example, towards the end of the growing season, the increase in dry mass slowly comes to a halt

at a time when the seeds are developing and increasing greatly in size with stored food. This is caused by a diversion of nutrients from leaves to seeds, the leaves dying in the process. By the rule of irreversible change in dry mass, plant growth has stopped. As already explained, dry mass may decline when a seed germinates until the seedling starts to photosynthesise.

SUMMARY

◆ Growth can be defined in a number of ways. The best general definition is an irreversible increase in dry mass of living material.

◆ Growth is closely linked with development, a progressive series of changes which includes cell specialisation (differentiation) and results in greater complexity.

◆ Growth is complex and cannot easily be measured by a single variable. Different methods are used, each with its own particular advantages and disadvantages. For example, increase in dimensions, dry or fresh mass, or cell numbers can be measured. Absolute growth (actual growth), absolute growth rate (change in rate of growth with time) or relative growth rate (which takes into account size) can be plotted as graphs known as growth curves.

◆ Different patterns of growth occur. For example, insects show two different types of metamorphosis.

◆ Microorganisms provide a useful simple model of population growth.

Questions

1 Explain what is meant by the terms growth and development.

2 Distinguish between
   a development and differentiation
   b individual growth and population growth.

3 Describe, giving full experimental details, how you could measure the absolute increase in dry mass of a plant from seed to maturity.

4 Name an insect showing complete metamorphosis. Outline four methods by which you could measure its growth and summarise the advantages and disadvantages of each method.

5 Growth may be measured as absolute growth, absolute growth rate or relative growth rate. Explain the advantages of each as a measure of growth.

6 Discuss the usefulness of unicellular organisms as models for population growth.

CHAPTER 2

Asexual reproduction

By the end of this chapter you should be able to:

1 review the range of organisms in which asexual reproduction is found;

2 describe asexual reproduction using one example from each of the five kingdoms: Prokaryotae, Protoctista, Fungi, Plantae and Animalia;

3 discuss the advantages and disadvantages of asexual reproduction as it occurs naturally and explain its evolutionary significance;

4 describe how knowledge of asexual reproduction, growth and development has been used commercially to develop methods of artificial propagation (cloning);

5 discuss the advantages and disadvantages of plant cloning.

Reproduction is the production of a new organism or organisms by an existing member or members of the same species. No living organism is immortal, so reproduction is essential for the renewal and survival of a species. This is the primary function of reproduction, but it is also the basis of population growth and spread.

Reproduction takes place in two ways, asexual and sexual. Some organisms use both methods, others just one.

> **Asexual (non-sexual) reproduction** is the production of new individuals from a single parent without the production of gametes.

It is particularly common in plants, simple animals and microorganisms. All the individuals produced by one parent are referred to as a **clone** and are genetically identical (*Biology 1*, chapter 6).

> **Sexual reproduction** is the fusion of two haploid gametes, usually a male and a female gamete, to form one diploid cell, the zygote.

This develops into a new organism. The gametes may come from one individual, or from separate male and female parents. Meiosis must be involved at some stage in the life cycle (*Biology 2*, chapter 4).

SAQ 2.1

Why must meiosis occur somewhere in the life cycle of an organism that reproduces sexually?

For some organisms, such as humans and other mammals, sexual reproduction is the only natural form of reproduction, although *artificial* cloning (a form of asexual reproduction) is now a possibility. Our concept of a species is linked to sexual reproduction because, by definition, a species is a group of organisms which can interbreed by sexual reproduction to produce fertile offspring (see *Biology 2*, chapter 5).

Both types of reproduction are widespread and have their own particular advantages and disadvantages. In this chapter we shall focus on asexual reproduction and its usefulness as a strategy for the long-term survival of a species. We shall also see how widespread a strategy it is, and how humans are increasingly able to make commercial use of the process.

The range of living organisms

It is not possible to understand the biological significance of asexual reproduction without first appreciating something of the huge variety of life on this planet. It is estimated that there are at least five million different species of living organisms, ranging from microscopic, single-celled types to the most complex multicellular plants and animals. The variety would be bewildering if we did not make some attempt to place organisms into groups, in other words to **classify** them. The most widely used classification system divides all organisms into five kingdoms (*figure 2.1* and *Biology 2*, chapter 5). Each of the five kingdoms contains organisms that reproduce asexually. Examples are shown in *figure 2.2*, and reviewed below.

Prokaryotes (bacteria)

Bacteria reproduce asexually by a process called **binary fission** (*figure 2.2a*). 'Fission' means division. 'Binary' refers to the fact that the cell divides into two. The two new cells are usually of equal size. Before the cell divides, the DNA replicates itself so that the two new cells have identical sets of genes. The process of DNA replication may be helped by an infolding of the plasma membrane which is thought to hold the DNA in position. This sometimes forms a more complex structure called the **mesosome**. In order to divide into two, the parent cell grows a new cell wall across the middle of the cell, as shown in *figure 2.2a*.

After division, the two daughter cells must grow to full size again before further division. At its most rapid, cell division can occur every 20 minutes in some species.

Protoctists

Protoctists include organisms which are thought to resemble the ancestors of modern plants, animals and fungi. Many are unicellular. They include the algae, a group of unicellular animal-like organisms called protozoa, and simple relatives of the fungi such as slime moulds. We will look at two simple examples of asexual reproduction from among the protozoa, namely *Amoeba* and *Paramecium*. *Amoeba* changes shape as it moves around in the same way as the white blood cells known as phagocytes (*Biology 1*, chapters 4 and 16). *Paramecium* is covered in fine hairs called cilia which bring about locomotion by beating. Both organisms grow to their mature size before undergoing binary fission. As in bacteria, the DNA replicates first, followed by cell division. In the case of *Amoeba* the cell divides transversely (across the middle), whereas *Paramecium* divides longitudinally (*figure 2.2b*). The daughter cells are genetically identical to the parent cell.

Fungi

Fungi are a large group of organisms, some of the more familiar of which are the yeasts, moulds, mildews, mushrooms and toadstools. Apart from the yeasts, which are unicellular, fungi have a characteristic body structure which is made up of a network of fine tube-like threads called **hyphae**. These may pack together into tissue-like structures, as in mushrooms and toadstools. A mass of hyphae is called a **mycelium**. If you have ever seen blue-green patches of mould on old bread, for example, each patch is a mycelium.

Prokaryotae (Prokaryotes)
bacteria
unicellular

Eukaryotes

Protoctista (Protoctists)
most unicellular eukaryotes and their simple multicellular descendants
mainly live in water

Animalia (Animals)
at least 3 million species they take in food from their environment and digest it inside their bodies
locomotion, heterotrophic

Fungi
about 80 000 species includes the yeasts, moulds, mushrooms etc. They secrete enzymes and digest food outside their bodies. Products of digestion are then absorbed.
no locomotion, heterotrophic

Plantae (Plants)
about 250 000 species they manufacture their own food by photosynthesis
no locomotion, photosynthetic, mainly live on land

● **Figure 2.1** The five kingdoms of living organisms (*Biology 2*, chapter 5). The difference between prokaryotes and eukaryotes is explained in *Biology 1*. Fungi and animals are heterotrophic – their source of carbon is organic. Plants are autotrophic – their source of carbon is inorganic (carbon dioxide). The prokaryotic and protoctist kingdoms contain a mixture of heterotrophic and autotrophic organisms.

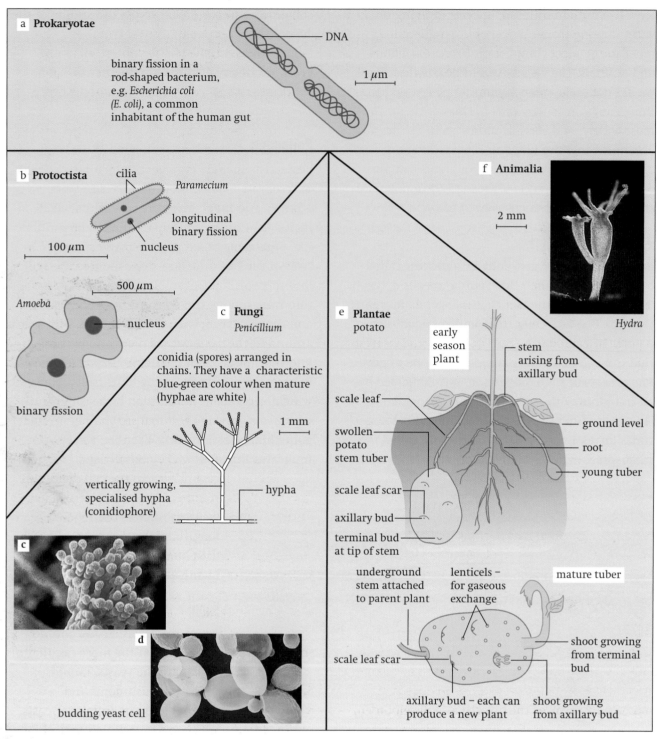

a Prokaryotae

DNA

binary fission in a
rod-shaped bacterium,
e.g. *Escherichia coli*
(E. coli), a common
inhabitant of the human gut

1 μm

b Protoctista

cilia

Paramecium

longitudinal
binary fission

nucleus

100 μm

500 μm

Amoeba

nucleus

binary fission

c Fungi

Penicillium

conidia (spores) arranged in
chains. They have a characteristic
blue-green colour when mature
(hyphae are white)

1 mm

vertically growing,
specialised hypha
(conidiophore)

hypha

c

d

budding yeast cell

e Plantae

potato

early
season
plant

scale leaf

swollen
potato
stem tuber

scale leaf scar

axillary bud

terminal bud
at tip of stem

underground
stem attached
to parent plant

lenticels –
for gaseous
exchange

scale leaf scar

axillary bud – each can
produce a new plant

stem
arising from
axillary bud

ground level

root

young tuber

mature tuber

shoot growing
from terminal
bud

shoot growing
from axillary bud

f Animalia

2 mm

Hydra

● **Figure 2.2** Examples of asexual reproduction from each of the five kingdoms. Each of these examples is
described in more detail in the text.

a Prokaryotae – a bacterium (*E. coli*) divides into two. Before dividing, the DNA of the cell replicates itself so
that each daughter cell is genetically identical to the parent cell. Each daughter cell grows to adult size
before dividing again. In the fastest-growing bacteria this may occur every 20 minutes, resulting in rapid
population growth (*figure 1.19*).

b Protoctista – binary fission in *Amoeba* and *Paramecium*.

c Fungi – diagram and scanning electron micrograph of *Penicillium* showing conidiophores and conidia
(spores) (× 9000).

d Fungi – scanning electron micrograph of budding yeast cells (× 1500).

e Plantae – potato.

f Animalia – *Hydra* budding (× 20) (see also *figure 2.3*).

Our first example of asexual reproduction in fungi is one of these blue-green moulds, called *Penicillium*. *Penicillium* grows on a wide range of substrates, from which it obtains nutrients. One species is the source of the antibiotic penicillin. Other species are used in the production of blue cheeses, such as roquefort. Fungi with hyphae, like *Penicillium*, reproduce asexually by means of **spores**. In *Penicillium* the spores are of a type known as **conidia**. They form at the tips of special, vertically growing hyphae called **conidiophores**. There is a characteristic brush-like arrangement of spores, as shown in *figure 2.2c*. The spores are coloured, giving the blue-green colour to the mature parts of the mycelium (the hyphae are white). The spores are light and small, just visible to the naked eye. They are therefore easily dispersed by air currents, and germinate to produce new hyphae when they land on a suitable medium. Their large numbers compensate for the high wastage of those that do not find a suitable medium.

Our second example of asexual reproduction in fungi is a yeast, chosen because it is easy to grow in laboratories and is also of commercial importance in brewing and baking. Yeasts are unusual fungi in being unicellular. They have a form of asexual reproduction known as **budding** (*figure 2.2d*) in which a new individual, identical to the parent, grows from the body of the parent. It starts as a bud and eventually breaks off. Budding also occurs in some plants and animals (see below).

Plants

Asexual reproduction occurs naturally on a widespread scale in the plant kingdom. The most common form is known as **vegetative propagation** and usually involves the growth and development of one or more buds on part of a stem to form a new plant. This eventually becomes detached from the parent and lives independently. Each bud contains a shoot apical meristem (chapter 1). Buds are found only on stems, so the organ of propagation must include at least a small piece of stem. The organs of propagation vary greatly in structure (e.g. bulbs, tubers and rhizomes), but they all have in common the fact that they contain a stem with buds. Even root tubers have a small piece of 'stem' with buds at their top ends.

Some common organs of propagation are described in *table 2.1*. In many cases these structures serve the equally important function of storing food for surviving adverse conditions such as winter or drought, to be used for growth when conditions become more suitable again.

A convenient organ of vegetative propagation to study in more detail is the potato tuber. A tuber is not just a means of propagation, but also stores food for overwintering. The potato tuber is a **stem tuber** as opposed to a root tuber (see below). Stem tubers are formed from a stem which grows underground and swells with food at its tip. The tuber possesses a bud at its tip, the **terminal bud**. This can grow out into a new shoot and eventually a new plant in the following growing season. The tuber is also covered with axillary buds which lie in the axils of the leaves. The leaves have not developed because the structure is underground. Each axillary bud may also grow into a new plant. Since each original potato plant can produce more than one underground stem and therefore more than one tuber, production of stem tubers is an effective means of reproduction and multiplication. Potato tubers in various stages of sprouting can usefully be examined in order to understand the location of buds and the fact that more than one shoot can be produced. Artificial cloning of potatoes is discussed later in this chapter.

Root tubers, such as dahlia and lesser celandine, are formed from roots which swell with food and have a bud where the root joins the stem. This bud acts as the terminal bud for next year's shoot.

Animals

Natural asexual reproduction in animals is confined to those which have a relatively simple structure. One such group of animals is the cnidarians. They include jellyfish, sea anemones, corals and *Hydra*, all of which show asexual reproduction in the form of budding. *Hydra* can be used as an example of how this is achieved (*figures 2.2f* and *2.3*). *Hydra* lives in freshwater, unlike most cnidarians, which live in the sea. It has a slender, hollow, cylindrical body up to 20 mm long, with long, thin, waving tentacles surrounding the single opening to the body, the mouth, at its tip.

Name of structure	Plant part	Location	Swollen with food for overwintering?	Notes	Examples
bulb	shoot	underground	yes	stem very short leaves swollen with food	daffodil (*Narcissus*) onion (*Allium*)
corm	stem	underground	yes	stem short	*Crocus, Gladiolus*
rhizome	stem	underground	sometimes, e.g. *Iris*	grows horizontally	mint (*Mentha*), couch grass (*Agropyron*)
stem tuber*	tips of stems or rhizomes	underground	yes		potato (*Solanum tuberosum*)
root tuber*	roots	underground	yes	buds just above root at base of old stem	*Dahlia*
swollen tap root	tap root (main root)	underground	yes	buds just above tap root at base of old stem	carrot (*Daucus*), swede (*Brassica napus*)
stolon	stem	above ground	no	arches over and touches ground. New roots and a new shoot grow from a bud at this point.	blackberry (*Rubus*), gooseberry (*Ribes*)
runner	stem	above ground	no	a type of stolon that elongates rapidly and tends to grow along the surface of the ground. It may be the main stem or grow from one of the lower buds on the main stem.	strawberry (*Fragaria*), creeping buttercup (*Ranunculus repens*)

* Unlike bulbs and corms, tubers survive only one year. The following year entirely new tubers are formed.

● **Table 2.1** Organs of vegetative propagation in plants.

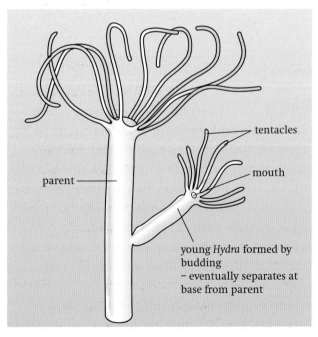

● **Figure 2.3** Budding of *Hydra*, a simple animal.

It anchors itself to something solid such as a stone or a water plant. The walls of its body consist of just two layers of cells. With such a simple body structure, budding is possible, whereas in more complex animals it does not occur. Buds usually start to grow towards the base of the body. Cells in both layers in this region multiply by mitosis and cell division, forming a hollow bulge in the wall. This increases in size, becoming cylindrical and eventually developing a mouth and tentacles. The new hydra can start feeding even before it breaks away from the parent. Eventually it is pinched off as a separate, genetically identical individual.

Another form of natural asexual reproduction in animals is **fragmentation**. Here the body breaks into two or more parts, each of which regenerates a new individual. Ribbon worms (phylum Nemertea), for example, are a group of simple, unsegmented marine worms with long, flattened bodies up to 20 metres in length. These bodies can break up naturally into pieces, each of which can regenerate. A common example, often found off European coasts, is *Tubulanus*, which may be up to half a metre long.

Artificial cloning of animals

The **artificial cloning** of animals is a form of asexual reproduction. The first successful cloning of a vertebrate from a mature adult cell was achieved in the late 1960s when Dr John Gurdon, who was working at Oxford University in the UK, developed a technique for cloning frogs from the skin or intestine cells of an adult frog *(Xenopus laevis)*. This involved removing skin or intestine cells and transplanting their diploid nuclei into the egg cells of a female frog. The haploid nuclei of the egg cells were first inactivated by ultraviolet radiation so that the new nuclei, already diploid, with instructions from the donor frog controlled development of the eggs. The tadpoles, and subsequent frogs, were genetically identical to the donor.

The first mammal to be cloned from a single specialised cell was Dolly the sheep in 1997. This technique has applications in both agriculture and medicine. Many copies of desirable animals may be produced in the future along with animals that have had human genes introduced into their genomes so that they produce otherwise expensive medical products such as hormones.

One form of animal cloning that is becoming important in animal breeding is the splitting of embryos at a very young stage when they consist of a ball of a few cells. Splitting an embryo once would create identical twins, but the process can be repeated many times to produce multiple clones. The clones can be grown in surrogate mothers. This technique has been used for cattle, sheep and goats.

The main application of animal cloning at present is not to produce many identical whole animals, but to maintain identical cells in culture (tissue culture) for a variety of purposes. For example, the effect on cells of new drugs, antibiotics and other pharmaceutical products, or cosmetics, can be tested without using whole animals. Cell cloning also has important applications in biotechnology. For example, some medically useful proteins, such as growth hormone, are in short supply and can be obtained from cloned mammalian cells. Research is continuing into improved methods of large-scale production. In the future cloning of human stem cells may provide a source of replacement tissues and organs, e.g. to treat nervous system diseases.

Advantages and disadvantages of natural asexual reproduction

The basis of asexual reproduction is mitosis. This is the division of a nucleus into two identical daughter nuclei. Each has the same genetic make-up because of the replication of DNA in interphase. After nuclear division, the rest of the cell divides, thus forming two genetically identical cells. (You may wish to refresh your memory of mitosis by reading *Biology 1* pages 83–5.) If all the cells so formed remain part of the same organism, the process is regarded as growth (chapter 1). However, if new organisms are formed, asexual reproduction has taken place. It follows that, as stated earlier, all the offspring (clones) produced by one parent as a result of asexual reproduction are genetically identical (*figure 2.4*).

Prokaryotes do not show mitosis in the same way as eukaryotes, but nevertheless their DNA also replicates before cell division.

Advantages and evolutionary consequences

- Only one parent is involved. This means that, in the case of organisms that move about (animals and some prokaryotes and protoctists), time and energy are not used in seeking a mate. For organisms that stay in one place, it avoids the problem of transferring gametes from one individual to another during sexual reproduction (for example cross-pollination, pages 42–4).
- There is no wastage of gametes. Production of gametes in sexual reproduction requires materials and energy and many gametes are inevitably wasted, particularly if released into water as, for example, in the case of many amphibians and fish, mosses and ferns.

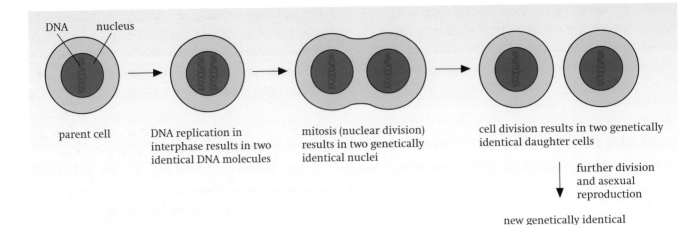

parent cell

DNA replication in interphase results in two identical DNA molecules

mitosis (nuclear division) results in two genetically identical nuclei

cell division results in two genetically identical daughter cells

further division and asexual reproduction

new genetically identical individuals (clones)

● **Figure 2.4** Mitosis and asexual reproduction.

■ Asexual reproduction can be effective in dispersing the species, possibly to exploit suitable habitats some distance from the parent where new resources are available. This is particularly important in fungi since they are non-motile but still need to reach new sources of food. In fungi, spores are commonly produced asexually and are ideal for dispersal by air currents since they are light and numerous.

■ Once an organism is established in a particular habitat, it may be able to spread more effectively in that habitat (i.e. colonise it) by asexual rather than sexual means. For example, grass plants and bracken can spread quite rapidly through an area by means of rhizomes (underground stems). Cord-grass (*Spartina townsendii*) is a common grass plant that grows on mudflats around the UK coast (*figure 2.5*). One reason why it is a very effective coloniser of fresh mud is its ability to send out new rhizomes through the mud, each of which can produce a new plant whilst still receiving nutrients from the established parent plant. Sea couch grass (*Agropyron pungens*) does the same on sand dunes.

■ Asexual reproduction can allow the rapid production of large numbers of offspring. New habitats can therefore be exploited rapidly. Microorganisms such as bacteria and fungi provide good examples of this.

■ Offspring are genetically identical to the parent. This has important evolutionary consequences because it can be an advantage for the offspring to have the same characteristics as the parent if

the latter is well adapted to its environment and is successfully competing with other organisms. Darwin's theory of natural selection states that the 'fitter' members of a species have a greater chance of survival. Asexual reproduction preserves successful combinations of alleles, an advantage if environmental conditions are stable.

Disadvantages and evolutionary consequences

■ The major disadvantage of asexual reproduction, and probably the reason why sexual reproduction evolved, is that no genetic variation occurs among the offspring. As we saw above, there are circumstances in which this may be an advantage. However, Darwin's theory also states that evolution proceeds by natural selection. This in

● **Figure 2.5** Asexual reproduction by rhizomes in *Spartina*, a grass plant which colonises mudflats and salt marshes.

turn depends on variation existing among the members of a species since the 'fitter' variants are the ones that are more likely to survive when there is some change in the environment. A good example of this was the introduction of the virus which causes myxomatosis into the rabbit population of Britain in 1952 (*Biology 2*, chapter 3). Although the virus was very effective at reducing the rabbit population, a few rabbits proved resistant and survived to multiply. After many years, the rabbit population developed a high level of resistance. The virus was originally obtained from Australia, and there the rabbit is now a major pest again, with a population estimated at 200–300 million. In 1994, tests began in Australia with a new virus to try to reduce the population again. This new virus, rabbit haemorrhagic virus, naturally emerged in China in 1984 and has since spread through four continents, killing hundreds of millions of rabbits. Unless there was genetic variation among rabbits, the species would be in danger of being wiped out completely. Sexual reproduction helps to increase variation within a population and ensures the long-term survival of the species.

■ If spores are produced, this may be wasteful of materials and energy since many do not find suitable conditions for germination. However, if such a method of reproduction has arisen as a result of evolution, the advantages of producing spores (see above) must outweigh the disadvantages for those species that produce them.

■ Asexual reproduction and consequent spread of an organism in one area can lead to overcrowding and exhaustion of resources such as nutrients (bacterial population growth, page 17).

In looking at the advantages and disadvantages of asexual reproduction, and comparing asexual with sexual reproduction, we are not trying to judge which is the better form of reproduction. Both can be successful strategies, depending on the circumstances. Both have certain advantages. Some organisms use both strategies, others have come to rely exclusively on just one. For example *Amoeba*, a one-celled protoctist, has never been observed to carry out sexual reproduction, and many animals, including humans, do not show asexual reproduction.

SAQ 2.2

Suggest four possible changes in the environment that could reduce the survival rate of a population of birds.

Artificial propagation (cloning) of plants

The origins of agriculture go back about 12 000 years, when people in the Middle East began to cultivate cereal crops and changed from a gatherer-hunter existence to a more settled way of life based on farming. Farming demanded a basic understanding of plant growth, development and reproduction. Although our knowledge of these processes has developed enormously since, it is still true today that improvements in our understanding of plant breeding are likely to lead to the more efficient use of plants for our own needs. Agriculture is now the world's largest industry in economic terms and current progress is rapid. Revolutionary new methods of propagating plants artificially have been developed over the last 30 years. Also, new food crops, and crops grown for expensive products such as drugs and perfumes, are being developed, and there are continuing efforts to genetically improve existing crops and the efficiency of their production. This is particularly true in the branch of agriculture known as **horticulture**, which is usually associated with the intensive production of high-value crops such as flowers, vegetables, shrubs and fruit trees.

We shall be looking here at how our knowledge of plant growth and development has been used commercially to develop methods of artificial propagation. A number of such methods exist, and are now considered in turn.

Cuttings

Taking cuttings is the most common 'traditional' method of artificial propagation. **Cuttings** are parts of plants removed by cutting that, when placed in suitable conditions, produce new roots and grow into new plants. The cutting may be a stem, leaf or root. Rooting hormone (an auxin, see chapter 5 and *Biology 2*, chapter 6) is sometimes added to stimulate rooting. Some plants which are commonly reproduced artificially in this way are: house plants such as *Pelargonium* and *Coleus*, in which the shoots are used as cuttings; *Forsythia*, a common shrub which produces yellow flowers in spring, in which the shoots (twigs) are used as cuttings; the African violet, another popular house plant, in which the leaves are used as cuttings; the blackcurrant, commercially important for the manufacture of fruit drinks, in which the shoots are used; and *Chrysanthemum*, a popular autumn flower, in which, again, the shoots are used.

Grafting and budding

Grafting is the transplantation of the upper part of one plant, the **scion**, onto the lower part of another, the **stock** (*figure 2.6*). The new plant usually has the root system of the stock and develops the shoot system of the scion. The stock is chosen for its vigour and the scion is usually chosen for its superior flowers or fruit. Sometimes the stock is chosen for its dwarfing effect, which generally makes trees bear fruit earlier. This is a common method of propagating those fruit trees, like apple, pear, peach and plum, which cannot easily be grown from cuttings. Most rose bushes are also propagated by this method since too much variation results from sexual reproduction. In the case of roses, buds are typically grafted onto vigorous woody stocks, such as the wild dog rose. When the scion is a single bud on a short portion of stem the technique is also known as **budding** (*figure 2.7*). (Note that *new* varieties have to be created by *sexual* reproduction.)

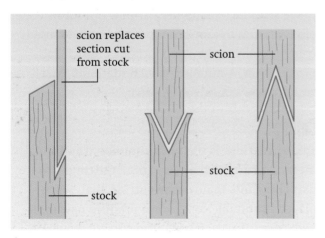

● **Figure 2.6** Grafting – three of the many ways of adding scion to stock.

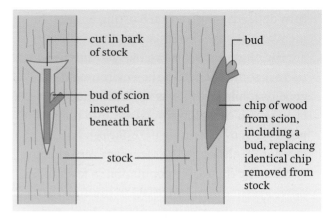

● **Figure 2.7** Budding – two methods.

Layering

Layering is another traditional method of propagation. It relies on the natural ability of many stems to produce roots when covered with soil. The stem is covered with soil while still attached to the parent plant, often by pegging a convenient section of stem just beneath the surface of the soil. Some examples are shown in *figure 2.8*.

Once new roots are well established, the stem can be cut and separated from the parent plant, thus creating a new plant. This can be transplanted to a new location if necessary. Root growth can be encouraged by a variety of methods, including the use of rooting hormone. It helps to make sure the relevant section of stem is not exposed to light. Some plants, such as strawberry, layer naturally by producing long horizontal stems called runners. These can root at nodes where buds grow into shoots. The runners can be arranged and pegged as convenient. The blackberry will also layer naturally (*figure 2.8*) as the tips of some shoots loop down and touch the soil.

Micropropagation (tissue culture)

'Micro' means small and 'propagation' means multiplying – in this case cloning. **Micropropagation** is the cloning of identical cells or small pieces of plant tissue, known as **explants**, in an artificial culture medium. The culture medium is usually in the form of a solution or agar gel containing nutrients and growth regulators. The growth of tissue under controlled conditions in this way is called **tissue culture**. The technique allows the rapid production of large numbers of genetically identical plants.

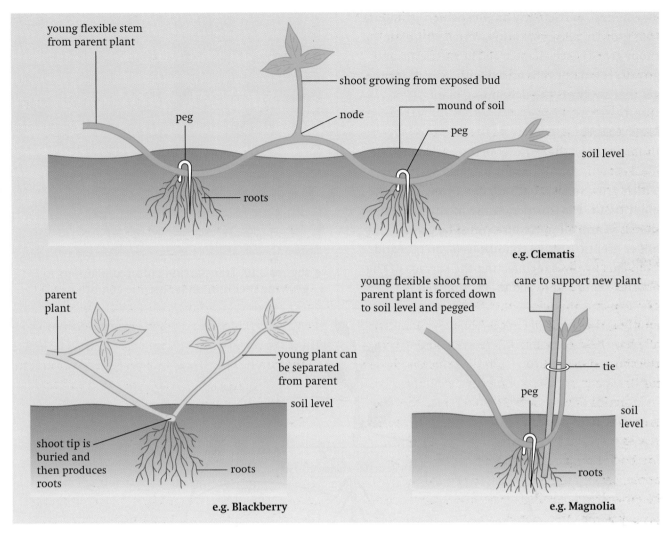

young flexible stem from parent plant

shoot growing from exposed bud

mound of soil

peg

node

peg

soil level

roots

e.g. Clematis

parent plant

young flexible shoot from parent plant is forced down to soil level and pegged

cane to support new plant

young plant can be separated from parent

soil level

tie

peg

soil level

shoot tip is buried and then produces roots

roots

roots

e.g. Blackberry

e.g. Magnolia

● **Figure 2.8** Three methods of layering.

An important step in the development of micro-propagation came in the 1960s when F.C. Steward of Cornell University in the USA grew whole new carrot plants from a few mature cells of carrot root, using a culture medium containing a special mix of nutrients and growth regulators. Steward had shown what had long been suspected, namely that individual specialised cells still had all the information (DNA) needed to control the production of a new plant. This property is referred to as **totipotency**, and is the basis of micropropagation. It is the same property that Gurdon discovered in specialised animal cells when working on frogs (see page 25) and which allows cloning of animals. The work of Steward and Gurdon convinced biologists that differentiation always involves switching on and off of genes rather than the loss of DNA.

An outline of the techniques involved in plant tissue culture is given below.

The culture medium

A typical culture medium contains sucrose as a source of energy, other organic nutrients such as amino acids and vitamins, and a wide range of inorganic ions such as nitrate, potassium, phosphate and trace amounts of iron and copper. It also contains a balance of growth regulators

● **Figure 2.9** Cutting up cultured tissue for planting as individual plantlets.

(hormones), particularly **auxins**, which stimulate root growth, and **cytokinins**, which stimulate shoot growth (see chapter 5). The nutrients and growth regulators are mixed with agar to form a gel that supports the developing plants.

Aseptic technique

Unfortunately, the culture medium also provides ideal growth conditions for bacteria and fungi, which grow so fast that they can overwhelm the plant tissue. For this reason the medium must be sterilised and all procedures must be carried out under aseptic (sterile) conditions (*figures 2.9* and *2.10*). This involves disinfecting the surface of the original plant tissue and preventing any

● **Figure 2.10** Transferring cultured plantlets to growing medium under aseptic conditions.

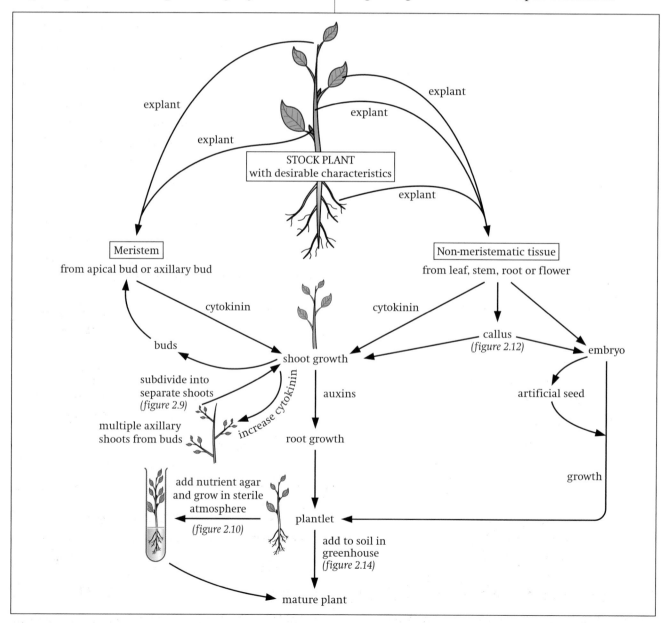

● **Figure 2.11** Methods of cloning from a stock plant.

subsequent contamination by growing the tissue culture in special, sealed transparent containers. These are placed in growth rooms where environmental conditions such as light and temperature are strictly controlled. All instruments used to handle the tissues are sterilised, and workers wear protective clothing.

Mass production

Figure 2.11 summarises the basic methods of cloning from a **stock plant**. (In this case, a stock plant is one that shows the desirable characteristics for cloning. Do not confuse this with the stock plants used in grafting.) *Figures 2.9, 2.10, 2.12–2.14* show some of the stages in micropropagation.

One or more stock plants must first be produced with the desired properties for cloning. Small pieces of tissue (explants) are taken from these as shown in *figure 2.11*. The most important method commercially is to start with meristematic tissue and develop many axillary shoots. This can be done by using a high concentration of the plant growth regulator cytokinin (chapter 5), which stimulates bud and shoot growth so that a short shoot with many branches is produced. This can later be subdivided into many plants (*figure 2.9*).

The other methods shown in *figure 2.11* have more particular uses. One of these is to produce a callus from non-meristematic (non-dividing) plant cells. A **callus** is a mass of disorganised and unspecialised cells. The callus can be induced to form roots or shoots by carefully balancing the amounts of auxin and cytokinin (growth regulators) in the medium (*figure 2.12*). Given the right conditions, cells from callus tissue or from non-

meristematic tissue sometimes behave as if they are zygotes and develop into embryos and then into plantlets (small plants, *figure 2.11*). Embryos can be embedded in pellets of alginate jelly to produce what is termed **artificial seed**.

SAQ 2.3
Explain why such material is referred to as artificial seed.

Once the growing tissues have produced new shoots, they can be subdivided to produce new plants. This is routinely done at regular intervals, typically every four to eight weeks (*figure 2.9*). In practice, the number of plants can sometimes be increased two- to four-fold every four to eight weeks and, over a year, thousands or even millions of identical plants can be created from one original culture. The young plantlets can be kept in cold storage to build up numbers before being grown in warmer conditions into mature plants. This build up is necessary if a bulk supply is required, for example for a new plantation of trees or the planting out of a crop at the right time of year.

Table 2.2 shows that the Netherlands, Europe's largest producer of micropropagated plants, produced over 61 million plants in 1988 by these methods. The majority were pot plants, cut flowers and ornamental corms and bulbs, such as tulips. Over two million orchids were produced. Large-scale

Type of product	Number of plants propagated
Ornamental plants	
pot plants, e.g. cyclamen	26 730 000
cut flowers	18 231 000
ornamental bulbs and corms	12 951 000
orchids	2 448 000
plants for aquaria	412 000
carnivorous plants	10 000
Trees and shrubs	
ornamental and fruit	193 000
Agricultural crops	
potato	395 000
sugar beet	37 000
rye grass	2000
vegetables	93 000
Total	61 502 000

● **Figure 2.12** Young shoots arising from callus tissue derived from an anther.

● **Table 2.2** Production of micropropagated plants in the Netherlands in 1988.

production of agricultural crops is less common, with the exception of potatoes, where micropropagation is used to produce virus-free plants. Potato plantlets are formed in large numbers from axillary shoot cultures as shown in *figure 2.11*. These then produce minitubers small potatoes which can be sown directly in fields and generate normal plants. More than half a million minitubers, can be produced from one original tuber in one year using micropropagation. At the end of the second year, the potato yield from these is over three million kilograms of tubers.

The UK has built up a sizeable export market in tropical and sub-tropical plantation crops such as banana, sugar cane, date and oil palms. Oil palms, in particular, have been produced in large numbers from callus tissues, allowing the production of unlimited numbers of stable, uniform types. *Figure 2.13* shows the mass production of orchids in Thailand and *2.14* a biotechnology greenhouse in Scotland.

Advantages of artificial propagation (cloning) of plants

The chief advantage of artificial propagation is that the cloned plants are genetically identical to the parent plant. Many copies of plants with desirable characteristics can therefore be produced. The selective breeding of plants, involving sexual reproduction, is probably as old as agriculture itself. However, it is difficult to produce true breeding lines when relying on sexual reproduction, particularly when

● **Figure 2.13** Commercial micropropagation. Rows of orchid cultures, each in a sterile atmosphere, in Bangkok, Thailand.

● **Figure 2.14** Plants grown in this biotechnology greenhouse in Dundee, Scotland experience ideal conditions for growth.

a plant is adapted for cross-pollination, such as the apple tree. Typically many generations of selection are necessary. By cloning, particular combinations of alleles can be fixed in just one step.

In some cases, cloning is simply a more *convenient* method of propagating plants than sowing seeds. Taking cuttings of blackcurrant bushes or layering strawberry runners, for example, are rapid and simple procedures, and cut out the need to nurture delicate seedlings. Some plants, such as the commercially grown banana, are sterile or suffer from low germination rates when propagated naturally. For other plants, such as orchids, it may be difficult to set up the correct conditions for successful seed germination. In these cases, cloning is a more practical alternative.

Tissue culture has particular benefits associated with it.

■ Rapid production of large numbers of plants from just one or a few stock plants can be achieved. This technique is increasing in use every year.

■ Plant diseases can be avoided. For example, virus-free plants can be obtained by selecting only meristematic tissue. Viruses tend to be distributed throughout the plant body by the vascular system, but the meristems lack vascular tissue and are therefore free of most viruses. They are usually also bacteria free. The meristem can subsequently be heat-treated to kill most or all remaining viruses and bacteria since they are usually more sensitive to heat than the meristematic cells. As already mentioned, micropropagation is important in the production of virus-free potatoes.

- Micropropagated plants can be produced at any time of year and can also be put in cold storage, taking up relatively little space. Combined with rapid production, this gives great flexibility in supplying consumer demand. Plants can be produced out-of-season and perhaps sold for higher prices as a result. New varieties of house and garden plants can be created quickly, introducing a fashion element into horticulture. A large and profitable market is opening up in which people can buy plants all year round at low prices in supermarkets.
- Many identical plants can be produced for subsequent plant breeding programmes that require sexual reproduction, for instance to produce new colours, scents, tastes.
- Exotic plants, such as orchids and insectivorous plants, that are hard to produce in large quantities from seed can be cloned in large numbers and sold at affordable prices.
- Micropropagation can be linked with genetic engineering. If a new gene is introduced into a plant cell by genetic engineering, the modified cell can be grown into a whole plant and then cloned to produce many new plants, all containing that gene.
- To some extent, plants can now be designed to order. The ornamental plant *Ficus*, for example, can be produced in a single-stemmed or a multi-stemmed form.
- Their light weight and small size mean that micropropagated plants can be airfreighted easily and cheaply, thus increasing international trade.
- Standardising the growing conditions produces batch after batch of standard plants. Such reliability and quality control is an important sales advantage.

SAQ 2.4
Suggest **a** two advantages and **b** two disadvantages of growing plants from bulbs rather than from seeds.

Disadvantages of artificial propagation (cloning) of plants

The main disadvantage of cloning is that it is not as convenient as sowing seed when very large numbers of plants are required, as it is so labour intensive. It would be desirable, for example, to produce certain vegetables such as carrots and celery by artificial propagation because these plants normally show cross-pollination, which can lead to undesirable variation. However, the planting out of sufficient identical seedlings would be too time-consuming and uneconomic compared with mechanical drilling of a large field with seeds.

Secondly, all the clones are genetically identical so any change in environmental conditions, or the appearance of a new disease, could have devastating consequences if the plants are not resistant or cannot adapt.

Tissue culture, in particular, has certain disadvantages associated with it:

- The processes are labour intensive and there are therefore high costs. In the future, it is likely that more automation will be introduced but the equipment needed is expensive. Individual plants must therefore have a high market value and this is why tissue culture is mainly confined to ornamental rather than crop plants (*table 2.2*).
- The work must be carried out in sterile conditions. This requires highly trained staff and imposes severe constraints on working practice.
- Since the techniques are relatively new, some unforeseen problems have arisen. For example, it was decided in the 1970s to the replace oil palms on Malaysian plantations with new micropropagated varieties. Five years later, when the first fruit (from which the palm oil is extracted) should have been produced, the plants were discovered to be sterile. The problem was traced to genetic changes that had taken place in the tissue culture. Such genetic changes seem to be a risk in tissue culture and strict quality controls are needed to avoid such problems.

SUMMARY

◆ Asexual reproduction is the production of new individuals from a single parent without the involvement of meiosis and gametes. Its basis is mitosis.

◆ Asexual reproduction occurs in all five kingdoms of living organisms.

◆ Methods of natural asexual reproduction vary and include fission (for example, bacteria and some protoctists), spore production (for example, many fungi), budding (for example, *Hydra* and yeasts), and various forms of vegetative propagation in plants.

◆ There are advantages in reproducing asexually. These include the need for only one parent and no wastage of gametes. In some species, asexually produced spores are used for dispersal. In some, rapid multiplication and spread is achieved asexually. Production of genetically identical offspring is an advantage where an individual is well adapted to a stable environment.

◆ Disadvantages of asexual reproduction include the possibility of overcrowding in an area and a lack of genetic variation among offspring. Genetic variation increases the survival chances of a species because it makes it more likely that some individuals will survive adverse changes in conditions such as a new disease or climate.

◆ Our knowledge of asexual plant propagation (cloning) has led to commercial exploitation of the process. Various methods are used, including cuttings, grafting, layering and, more recently, tissue culture (micropropagation).

◆ Tissue culture is of great commercial importance. It is used particularly for producing flowers, ornamental plants and virus-free potatoes.

◆ Cloning allows mass production of identical, disease-free plants selected for their ideal characteristics. Plants can be put into long-term storage and produced at any time of year. More flexibility in creating new varieties and meeting consumer demands is possible.

◆ Cloning of some plants is not practicable. Tissue culture is labour intensive, relatively expensive and requires sterile operating conditions. Some unexpected problems arise from time to time because techniques are new. Cloned plants are genetically identical, so all plants are equally vulnerable to new diseases or environmental change.

Questions

1 a Discuss the commercial advantages of cloning plants.
  b Discuss the possible disadvantages associated with cloning.

2 Define:
  a asexual reproduction;
  b sexual reproduction.
  Discuss the advantages of both types of reproduction.

3 Review, giving named examples, the range of methods used by animals and plants to carry out asexual reproduction under natural conditions.

4 Explain how mass production of plants can be achieved by artificial means.

5 Explain the need for the following, in work with tissue cultures:
  a growth regulators;
  b aseptic techniques.

Sexual reproduction in flowering plants

By the end of this chapter you should be able to:

1 recognise and name the main parts of a typical flower;

2 describe anther structure and pollen formation;

3 describe the development of the ovule;

4 distinguish between *self-pollination* and *cross-pollination*;

5 describe and explain the structural features of a typical insect-pollinated and a typical wind-pollinated flower;

6 explain the relative merits of self-pollination and cross-pollination;

7 describe mechanisms favouring cross-pollination and self-pollination;

8 describe double fertilisation in the embryo sac, and explain its significance;

9 carry out an experiment to observe pollen tube growth;

10 describe development of the ovule into the seed, including embryo development;

11 describe development of the ovary into the fruit;

12 carry out an experiment to investigate embryo development in shepherd's purse;

13 describe epigeal and hypogeal germination.

Sexual reproduction is the production of a new organism or organisms in a way that involves the production of gametes with one set of chromosomes (haploid) and their fusion to form a **zygote** with two sets of chromosomes (diploid). At some stage in the life cycle, **meiosis** must occur in order to prevent the number of chromosomes doubling every generation (*Biology 2*, chapter 4). Sexual reproduction has important evolutionary consequences because it brings two separate sets of chromosomes together and thereby generates genetic variation among the offspring. *Figure 3.1* shows a simplified life cycle of a plant, stressing the alternation of meiosis and fertilisation, which create haploid and diploid stages respectively. The role of **mitosis** in allowing growth is also highlighted.

In flowering plants, male and female gametes are produced in special structures, the **flowers**, which are unique to this group of plants. *Figure 3.2* shows a more detailed outline of the life cycle of a flowering plant. You will see that male gametes are made inside **pollen grains** (the pollen grain is not itself the gamete), and female gametes inside structures known as **embryo sacs**. In this chapter, we shall be looking at the different stages of this life cycle, so *figure 3.2* should be referred to from time to time to keep an overview of the whole process.

The parts of a flower

It is very helpful to be familiar with the main parts of a flower before trying to understand the life cycle of a flowering plant. The wallflower,

Cheiranthus cheiri, is a good example to study because it has a simple flower which is available relatively early in the year (March to June). It is in the same flowering family as shepherd's purse, which is studied later in this chapter.

The flowers are **hermaphrodite**, that is, they have both male and female parts. *Figure 3.3* shows the structure of its flower, and the following are some notes relating to flower structure.

- **Inflorescence** – a group of flowers on one stalk (the peduncle).
- **Pedicel** – the stalk of the flower. The top of the pedicel is swollen to form the receptacle.
- **Receptacle** – the petals and sepals grow from the receptacle.
- **Petals** – modified leaves arranged in a ring round the receptacle. They are often large and brightly coloured to attract insects for pollination. They are usually inconspicuous or absent in wind-pollinated flowers. The ring of petals is called the **corolla**. (Wallflower has four petals.)
- **Sepals** – modified leaves which form a ring outside the petals. They are usually green and leaflike, and close around and protect the flower bud. In some flowers, sepals resemble petals. The ring of sepals is called the **calyx**. (Wallflower has four sepals.)
- **Perianth** – the combined name for the sepals and petals (calyx and corolla).
- **Nectaries** – glandular structures from which a sugary liquid called nectar is

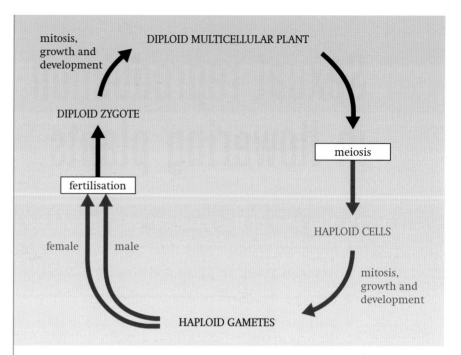

● **Figure 3.1** Simplified life cycle of a plant showing alternation of meiosis and fertilisation, haploid and diploid stages.

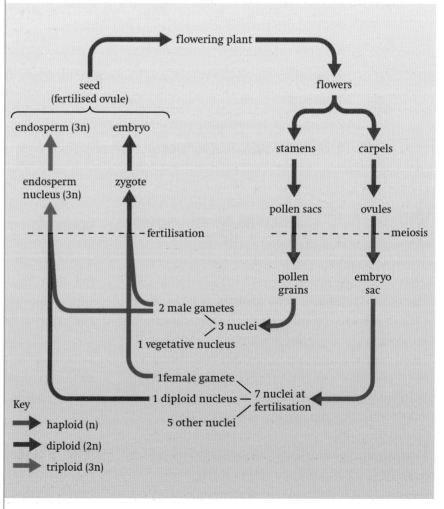

● **Figure 3.2** Life cycle of a flowering plant.

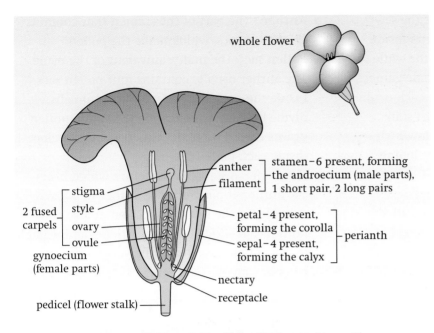

Flower is about 2.5 cm diameter. It is pollinated by bees and hoverflies. Petals are usually brightly coloured and fragrant.

● **Figure 3.3** Half-flower of wallflower (*Cheiranthus cheiri*). The female parts of the plant (carpels) are known collectively as the gynoecium; the male parts (stamens) as the androecium.

secreted. This attracts the animals, usually insects, that bring about pollination. They are found at the base of petals and/or sepals.

■ **Gynoecium** – the female reproductive parts of the flower, consisting of one or more carpels.

■ **Carpel** – basic unit of the gynoecium. Like petals and sepals, carpels probably evolved from leaves. Each carpel corresponds to a single leaf which is rolled up to form an enclosed chamber, the ovary. It is divided into three regions, the stigma, style and ovary (*figure 3.4*). The carpels of a flower may be separate, as in the buttercup, or united to form a single structure, as in the wallflower. (The wallflower has two fused carpels.)

■ **Stigma** – the tip of a carpel. Pollen grains become attached to the stigma during pollination. Its surface secretes a sugary fluid which stimulates germination and growth of pollen grains. It is usually at the end of a stalk-like structure called the style. (Wallflower has a stigma which is split into two, reflecting the fact that there are two carpels.)

■ **Style** – a stalk-like extension of the ovary which has the stigma at its tip. Its function is to

ensure that the stigma is in a position favourable for receiving pollen. Where the carpels are united, the styles may also be united to form one style, as in the wallflower, or stay separate, with separate stigmas.

■ **Ovary** – a **simple ovary** is the swollen base of a single carpel. It contains a chamber, the **locule**, in which one or more ovules are found (*figure 3.4*). A **compound ovary** is formed by the fusion of the bases of two or more carpels. It may contain one united cavity, or several cavities corresponding to the original separate carpels. (The wallflower has a compound ovary which contains many ovules inside a single chamber (locule), but the locule is divided into two by the growth of a 'false' wall down the middle.) In some species the ovary develops just *above* the receptacle, in which case it is called a **superior ovary**; in some it develops just *below* the receptacle, in which case it is called an **inferior ovary**.

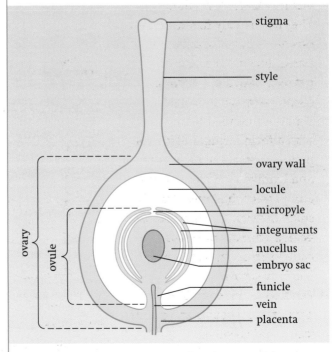

● **Figure 3.4** A carpel consisting of a stigma, style and ovary. The ovary contains one ovule in this case.

■ **Ovule** – the structure which becomes the seed after fertilisation. One or more is found inside the ovary. Meiosis takes place inside the ovule to produce a haploid **embryo sac**. A **female gamete** later develops inside the embryo sac. Each ovule is attached to the ovary wall by a short stalk called the **funicle**. This contains a vein which brings water and nutrients to the developing ovule. The point of attachment to the ovary wall is called the **placenta**. The ovule is protected on the outside by two layers, called **integuments**, which are continuous except for a tiny hole, the **micropyle**, at the tip of the ovule. The main body of the ovule, which is made of diploid parent cells, is called the **nucellus**. One of these cells later divides by meiosis to form the embryo sac, inside which a female gamete develops.

■ **Androecium** – the male reproductive parts of the flower, consisting of a collection of stamens.

■ **Stamen** – basic unit of the androecium. Like petals, sepals and carpels, stamens probably evolved from leaves. The stamen is usually divided into two parts, the anther and filament. (The wallflower has six stamens: an outer pair and two inner pairs.)

■ **Anther** – the part of the stamen that contains the pollen sacs, which make the pollen.

■ **Pollen sac** – the male equivalent of the ovule. The anther usually contains four pollen sacs. Inside the pollen sacs, diploid parent cells divide by meiosis to form four haploid **pollen grains** each. Two **male gametes** later develop inside each pollen grain.

■ **Filament** – a stalk-like structure which bears the anther. It positions the anther in a place suitable for the release of pollen. It also contains a vein which carries nutrients and water to the pollen sacs. (In wallflower the two inner pairs of stamens have longer filaments than the outer pair.)

Development of pollen grains

Pollen grains are formed inside the anthers in structures called pollen sacs (*figures 3.5* and *3.6*). Within the pollen sacs are many **pollen mother cells** which, like the other cells of the flowering plant, have diploid nuclei (two sets of chromosomes). Each mother cell divides by meiosis to form four haploid cells, each with only one set of chromosomes. At first the four cells are grouped together, forming a **tetrad**. Later, they separate and develop into pollen

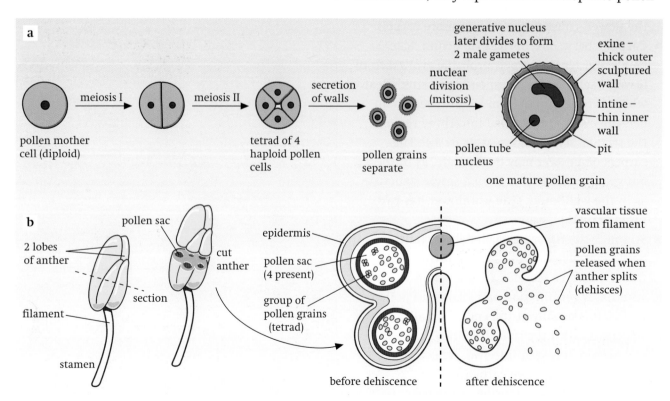

● **Figure 3.5 a** Development of pollen grains.   **b** TS anther before and after dehiscence.

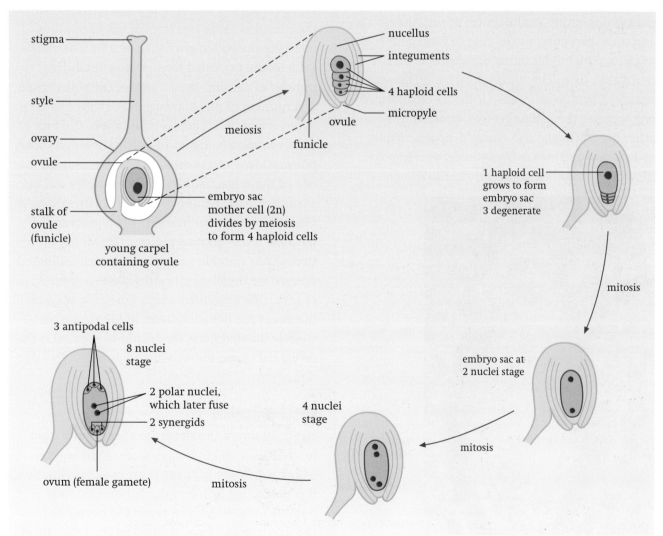

• **Figure 3.6** Photomicrograph of TS anther of *Lilium* before dehiscence (left-hand side) and after dehiscence (right-hand side).

grains (*figure 3.5a*). Each pollen grain has a thick, sculptured outer wall, the **exine**, the pattern being characteristic of the species or genus. The exine is made of an extremely resistant chemical called sporopollenin which can enable pollen grains to survive for long periods.

The pollen grain nucleus divides into two by mitosis forming a **generative nucleus**, which later divides to form two male gametes, and a **pollen tube nucleus** (*figure 3.5b*) all of which are haploid. The structure of the anther and development of the pollen can be observed in sections of mature anthers (*figures 3.5 and 3.6*). When the pollen is mature, the anthers dry, split open and release the pollen in a process termed **dehiscence**.

• **Figure 3.7** Development of the ovule to just before fertilisation.

Development of the ovule

This is best summarised by means of diagrams (*figure 3.7*). Inside the ovary are one or more ovules. Each ovule is attached to the ovary wall by a short stalk, the funicle, and is surrounded by protective integuments, usually two. A small pore, the **micropyle**, occurs in the integuments. The rest of the tissue of the ovule is known as the **nucellus**. One of the cells of the nucellus gives rise to the embryo sac and is known as the **embryo sac mother cell**. The remaining cells of the nucellus act as food for the developing embryo sac and quickly disappear. The nucleus of the embryo sac mother cell divides by meiosis to form four haploid nuclei within four cells. Three of these cells degenerate and die. One becomes the **embryo sac**. The embryo sac nucleus divides three times by mitosis to form eight nuclei, four at each end of the embryo sac. One nucleus from each end migrates to the centre of the embryo sac and these two polar nuclei fuse to form a diploid nucleus, which later forms the endosperm. The remaining six nuclei, three at each end, become separated by thin cell walls. Of the six cells formed, one becomes the female gamete, or **ovum**. The other five (antipodal and synergid) appear to have no function and eventually disintegrate. *Figure 3.8* shows an embryo sac just before fertilisation.

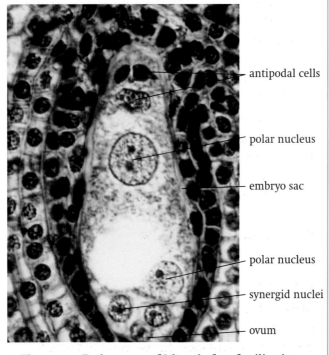

antipodal cells

polar nucleus

embryo sac

polar nucleus

synergid nuclei

ovum

● **Figure 3.8** Embryo sac of *Lilium* before fertilisation.

Pollination

Pollination is the transfer of pollen grains from the anther to the stigma.

Self-pollination is transfer to a stigma on the same flower or to a different flower on the same plant.

Cross-pollination is transfer to a stigma on another plant.

Do not confuse pollination with fertilisation! Pollination is necessary in order to bring the two male gametes, which are inside the pollen grain, to within close proximity of the female gamete so that fertilisation can take place. When anthers are mature, they dry and split open (**dehisce**) down their lengths along two lines of weakness, thus releasing the pollen grains (*figure 3.5b*). The male gametes are protected from drying out during transfer to a stigma by the wall of the pollen grain.

A number of mechanisms have evolved to help to ensure successful cross-pollination, the two most common being **wind pollination** and **insect pollination**. Flowers are often highly adapted for one of these mechanisms. Two examples will be examined here, namely white deadnettle (*Lamium album*) for insect pollination, and a grass called meadow fescue (*Festuca pratensis*) for wind pollination. Other suitable examples of insect-pollinated flowers are the bluebell (which flowers from April to June), the hyacinth (which flowers in May) or the sweet pea (which flowers in July). Another wind-pollinated grass that could be studied is the cereal oat (*Avena sativa*), which has relatively large flower parts.

Insect pollination

Figure 3.9 shows the structure of the white dead-nettle flower and indicates some of the ways in which the flower is adapted for insect pollination. It is pollinated by long-tongued insects, such as bumble bees, which can reach the nectaries from the 'landing platform' formed by the lower lip of the flower. The nectaries secrete nectar, a liquid

upper lip of corolla (2 petals) contains stamens and style. These are positioned to touch the bee's back as it enters the flower

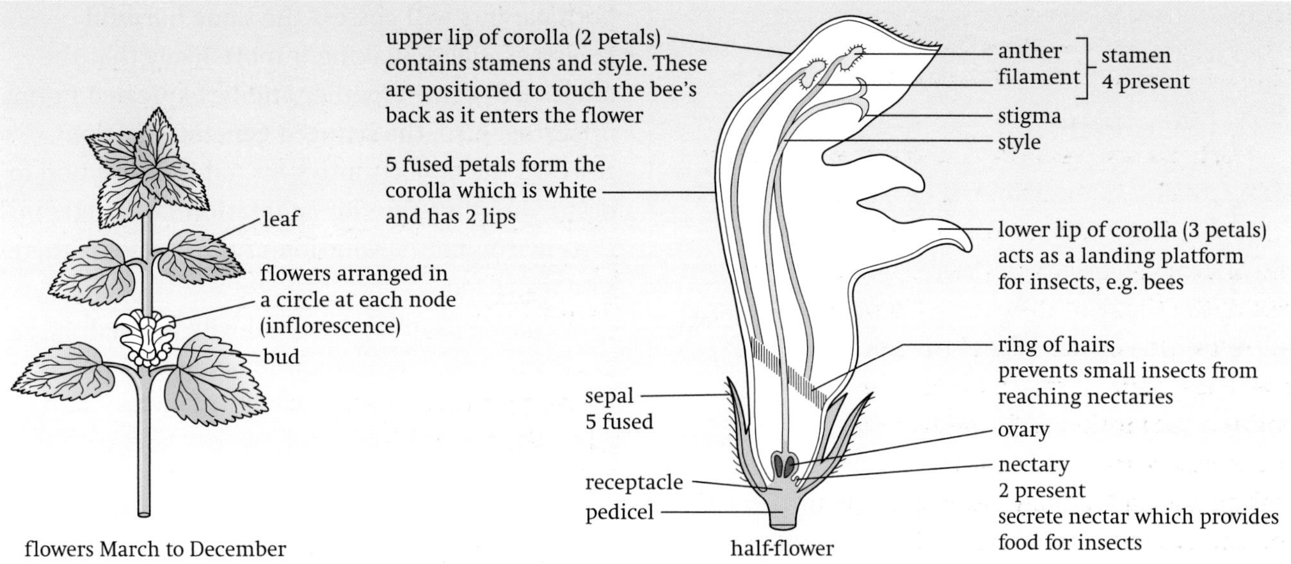

5 fused petals form the corolla which is white and has 2 lips

leaf

flowers arranged in a circle at each node (inflorescence)

bud

anther
filament

stamen
4 present

stigma
style

lower lip of corolla (3 petals) acts as a landing platform for insects, e.g. bees

ring of hairs prevents small insects from reaching nectaries

ovary

sepal
5 fused

nectary
2 present
secrete nectar which provides food for insects

receptacle

pedicel

flowers March to December

half-flower

● **Figure 3.9** White deadnettle, an insect-pollinated flower.

rich in sugars, amino acids and other nutrients, which the bees feed on. (They may also collect pollen for food.) The stigma projects below the anthers, so as the bee enters the flower its back touches the stigma first. Its back may be carrying pollen from a previous visit to another deadnettle flower. Pollination occurs when pollen from the back of the bee is transferred to the stigma. This will usually be cross-pollination, although the bee may bring pollen from another flower on the same planting, causing self-pollination. Next, the anthers touch the bee's back, shedding pollen onto it. To make cross-pollination more likely, the anthers mature before the stigma, ensuring that the stigma will not pick up the pollen just shed by the anthers. Also, the cluster of relatively large white flowers is conspicuous amongst green vegetation, helping to attract the bees.

The features mentioned here are characteristic of the white deadnettle. Other features that favour insect pollination may occur in other plants. For example, the stigma is usually sticky, making it more likely that pollen from the insect's body will attach itself. Many flowers have attractive scent and many have 'honey guides', conspicuous markings on the flower which guide insects to the nectaries.

Wind pollination

Figure 3.10 shows the structure of the meadow fescue flower, which is similar to that of most

grasses. Meadow fescue flowers are very small and inconspicuous, since they have not evolved to attract insects. Instead, pollination is by means of the wind. There are no petals, nectaries or scent to attract insects. However, the stigma is relatively large and feathery and is an effective pollen trap. The stamens hang outside the flowers when ripe and can swing freely in air currents. They produce large quantities of small, light pollen grains that have smooth surfaces and are easily dispersed by air currents. The flowers are borne on tall, loose, nodding inflorescences that also catch the wind easily. The chances of successful wind pollination are further increased by the fact that grasses, like most wind-pollinated plants, tend to live close to one another. However, wind pollination is more dependent on chance, and therefore more wasteful of pollen, than is insect pollination.

When examining grass flowers, the use of a hand lens or dissecting microscope and one or two dissecting needles are recommended since the flowers are very small and have to be carefully removed from surrounding leaf-like structures. Most grasses flower during May, June and July, as hay fever sufferers will know!

SAQ 3.1

Make a table to compare the adaptations for pollination shown by flowers of the white deadnettle (insect pollinated) and meadow fescue (wind pollinated).

spikelet
5–14 flowers in
each spikelet

arrangement of
spikelets in
inflorescence

30–120 cm high forming
tussocks. Often abundant
in water-meadows,
low-lying grassland, old
pastures and roadsides

stigma
feathery to trap
wind-blown pollen

anther
(3–4 mm long)

stamen

filament

ovary

filament allows
anther to tilt and
shake independently

each flower is enclosed by small
leaf-like structures not shown here

● **Figure 3.10** Meadow fescue, a wind-pollinated
flower.

The relative merits of self- and cross-pollination

We have seen that insect and wind pollination are
both ways of achieving cross-pollination and that
self-pollination is possible in some flowers. There
are advantages associated with both self- and
cross-pollination. In fact, many plant species show
both types.

Self-pollination has the advantage that it is very
reliable, particularly if the plants are widely
scattered. It is also advantageous in harsh environments, such as high on mountains where insects
and other pollinators are scarce. The major
disadvantage of self-pollination is that it results
in less genetic variation (see detail below). Self-
fertilisation occurs, with gametes from the same
parent fusing. This is an extreme form of
inbreeding, that is sexual reproduction between
genetically similar individuals (see *Biology 2*,
chapter 4). Inbreeding makes it more likely that

both parents will possess the same harmful
recessive alleles, making it more likely that the
alleles will come together and be expressed in the
offspring. Also, the reduced genetic variation
restricts the opportunities for natural selection to
occur, and therefore for adaptation to changes in
the environment. Evolution of the species is therefore restricted.

Before we examine in detail why inbreeding
results in less genetic variation, you may find it
useful to apply some knowledge of meiosis and
genetics that you should previously have gained to
the following question.

SAQ 3.2

The diploid cells of a given plant are all genetically
identical, as already noted in chapter 1. Pollen
mother cells and embryo sac mother cells are therefore all genetically identical. *Figure 3.11* shows a cell
with three pairs of chromosomes.

One of the chromosomes is carrying a harmful
recessive allele. When the nucleus divides by meiosis, independent assortment of chromosomes results
in genetically different gametes. Eight types of
gamete are possible.

a Draw eight circles and inside them draw chromosomes to show the eight genetically different
types of gamete that could be produced as a
result of independent assortment.

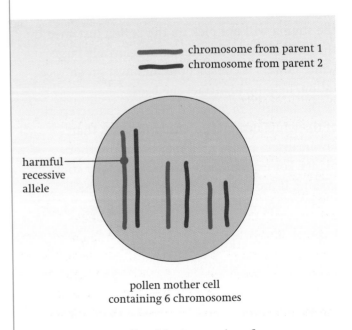

chromosome from parent 1
chromosome from parent 2

harmful
recessive
allele

pollen mother cell
containing 6 chromosomes

● **Figure 3.11** Cells with three pairs of
chromosomes.

b How many genetically different types of offspring could be produced by a plant that produces these gametes and undergoes self-fertilisation?

c What proportion of the gametes you drew in **a** would contain the harmful recessive allele?

d What proportion of the offspring of self-fertilisation would be homozygous for the recessive allele, and would therefore suffer from the harmful condition?

e What proportion of the offspring would be homozygous for the recessive allele if cross-pollination took place with a plant that did not possess the harmful allele?

f State two other processes in addition to independent assortment of chromosomes which could in practice increase the genetic variation among the offspring of a parent undergoing self-fertilisation.

g Explain why it makes no difference genetically whether self-pollination takes place in the same flower that produced the pollen or in another flower on the same plant.

h Summarise briefly how self-pollination differs from asexual reproduction and cross-pollination in its genetic consequences.

Cross-pollination is a form of **outbreeding**, that is sexual reproduction between genetically different individuals – the more genetically different, the greater the outbreeding. The advantage of cross-pollination is that it results in more genetic variation than self-pollination. As explained in *Biology 2*, this improves the chances of the species surviving environmental change and adapting well to its environment because it provides more variants for natural selection.

Cross-pollination results in greater genetic variation for the simple reason that the gametes are produced by genetically different individuals, and therefore show more genetic variation. For example, imagine a gene for height that exists in two alleles, a dominant allele **T**, tall and a recessive allele **t**, dwarf. If a parent is homozygous for the **t** allele, then all its gametes would carry the **t** allele and all the offspring would be dwarf if self-fertilisation took place. However, if cross-fertilisation took place, the second parent could be carrying the **T** allele, resulting in gametes carrying the **T** allele and some tall plants among the offspring.

Other factors increase the amount of variation obtained by cross-fertilisation. Some genes, for example, exist in more than two alleles, that is multiple alleles (*Biology 2*). This increases variation within the population as a whole. However, since a given individual can only possess two of the possible alleles, *self*-fertilisation would restrict variation. Another factor to bear in mind is that cross-pollination shuffles the alleles in the whole population every generation, whereas repeated self-fertilisation can only shuffle the alleles of the original parent in every generation.

The major disadvantage of cross-pollination is that it is less reliable. Plants can compensate to some extent by producing more pollen, but this is in itself a disadvantage in that more valuable resources are wasted as a result.

Mechanisms favouring cross-pollination

We have seen that cross-pollination brings genetic advantages and that elaborate mechanisms exist to increase the likelihood and efficiency of cross-pollination. The main ones are listed here but other, often unique, mechanisms can be found.

■ **Dioecious plants**. When a species, such as willow, produces separate male and female plants it is described as **dioecious**. Self-pollination is impossible in such species, but the number of dioecious plant species is very few. They are often trees: holly, yew and poplar are other examples.

■ **Monoecious plants**. Monoecious species, such as oak and birch, are those which produce separate male and female flowers on the *same* plant. This encourages cross-pollination between adjacent plants, while still allowing self-pollination among the flowers of the same plant.

■ **Protandry** and **protogyny**. Anthers and stigmas sometimes mature at different times, thus encouraging cross-pollination. If the anthers mature first, as in the white deadnettle, it is known as **protandry**. The term used when the stigmas mature first, as in the bluebell, is **protogyny**. Usually there is an overlapping period when both anthers and stigmas are ripe, allowing for self-pollination as well.

■ **Self-incompatibility**. Even if self-pollination occurs, self-*fertilisation* is often made less likely

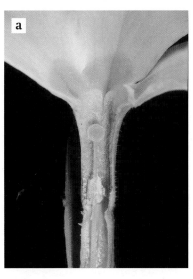

● **Figure 3.12** Cross-pollination in primrose. Two types of flower occur: **a** pin-eyed and **b** thrum-eyed.

or impossible by slow or zero growth of the pollen tubes. This is termed **incompatibility** and is genetically determined. An extreme example is clover, which is totally self-incompatible.

■ **Special structures**. *Figure 3.12* shows a special mechanism which favours cross-pollination in the primrose (*Primula vulgaris*). In this species, self-incompatibility also occurs.

SAQ 3.3

Examine *figure 3.12* which shows pin-eyed and thrum–eyed flowers of primrose. These are found on separate plants. **a** In one type of flower, the stigma is above the anthers and in one type below. Which is which? **b** Suggest how this favours cross-pollination by bees.

Mechanisms of self-pollination

Self-pollination is very common and can occur in probably more than half of all flowering plant species. Where it occurs, flowers are usually **hermaphrodite** (meaning that they have both male and female parts). A simple mechanism of self-pollination is for anthers and stigmas to mature at the same time and for the pollen to be shed directly onto the stigma. Flowers adapted for self-pollination are usually small, inconspicuous and produce no nectar or scent since they do not need to attract insects. Examples are groundsel and chickweed, both common weeds. In some

species or individual flowers, cross-pollination is physically prevented because the flower buds never open.

Fertilisation

If a pollen grain lands on the stigma of a compatible species, it will germinate (also see page 48). A pollen tube emerges from one of the pores (pits) in the pollen grain wall (*figures 3.5a* and *3.13* and *box 3.1*) and, responding to chemicals secreted by the ovary, grows rapidly down the style to the ovary (*figure 3.13*). This is an example of **chemotropism**, that is growth towards a chemical stimulus. Growth is controlled by the haploid **tube nucleus** which is found at the tip of the pollen tube. During growth, the haploid **generative nucleus** of the pollen grain divides by mitosis into two haploid nuclei, which are the male gametes (*figure 3.13*).

The pollen tube enters the ovule through the micropyle, the tube nucleus degenerates and the tip of the tube bursts, releasing the two male gametes. One fuses with the ovum (the female gamete) to form the diploid **zygote**. The other fuses with the diploid nucleus at the centre of the embryo sac to form a **triploid** nucleus, that is a

Box 3.1
Experiment to observe pollen tube growth
It is possible to investigate the germination of pollen grains using the dehiscing anthers of flowers such as wallflower, white deadnettle, *Pelargonium* or *Impatiens*, as follows.

The pollen grains need to be suspended in a 10% sucrose solution in the central depression of a cavity slide to stimulate germination.

The sucrose solution should contain borate at a concentration of 0.01% (to stimulate growth and help to prevent osmotic bursting of the pollen tube tips).

A drop of acetocarmine or neutral red can be used to stain the nuclei at the tip of the growing pollen tubes.

Once the pollen grains are growing, a microscope with a calibrated eye-piece can be used to measure the lengths of several of the tubes at appropriate intervals (e.g. every three minutes) and thus the rate of growth. The effects of sucrose concentration on the growth rate can also be studied, e.g. by measuring how the rate of growth changes when 20% sucrose solution is used instead.

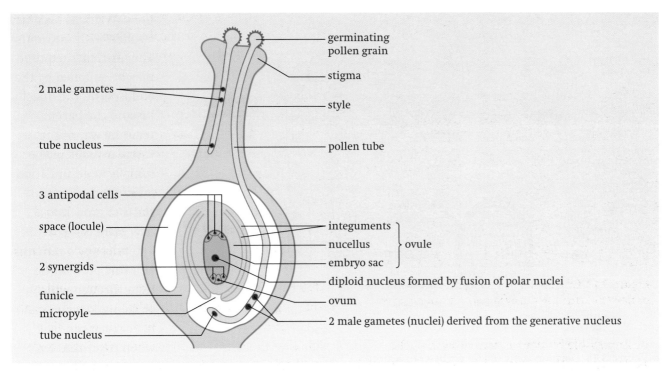

● **Figure 3.13** LS carpel at fertilisation.

nucleus with three sets of chromosomes. It is known as the **endosperm nucleus**. Thus a **double fertilisation** takes place, a process unique to flowering plants. The zygote will later grow to form the embryo, which will, in turn, grow into the next generation of the plant. The endosperm nucleus will often grow to form a food store in the seed (see below).

SAQ 3.4
Summarise the roles played by the two pollen grain nuclei.

SAQ 3.5
The male gametes of simple plants such as mosses and ferns are swimming sperm. Suggest why plants evolved a mechanism for carrying male gametes in pollen grains.

Development of the embryo and seed
Immediately after fertilisation, the ovule is re-termed the **seed**. Thus

a seed is a fertilised ovule.

The following changes take place during development of the seed (you will need to refer to *figures 3.7, 3.14–3.16* when studying these). The example chosen to illustrate the changes in detail is shepherd's purse.

1 The integuments become the **testa**. This is a thin, tough, layer around the seed. It protects the seed from mechanical damage and also often contributes to the dormancy mechanism as described in chapter 5.

2 The **nucellus** disintegrates as the seed develops, supplying nutrients for growth of the embryo and the endosperm in endospermous seeds (see below).

3 The triploid **endosperm nucleus** divides repeatedly by mitosis to form the triploid **endosperm**. The nuclei become separated from one another by thin cell walls. In some seeds (**endospermous seeds**) such as cereals, this remains as the food store for the seed. In **non-endospermous seeds** such as the pea and shepherd's purse, the cotyledons (see below) grow at the expense of the endosperm, which may then disappear altogether.

4 The **zygote** grows by repeated mitotic divisions to become an **embryo** and a **suspensor** with a 'basal cell' at its base. The suspensor is a short

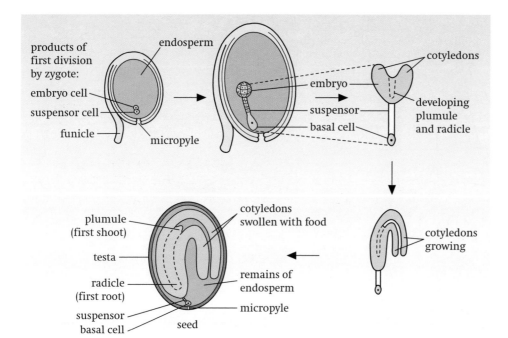

Figure 3.14 Development of the embryo in a non-endospermous dicotyledonous seed such as shepherd's purse (*Capsella bursa-pastoris*).

stalk consisting of just a few cells that elongate to push the embryo further into the embryo sac. The embryo consists of a **plumule** (the first shoot), a **radicle** (the first root) and either one or two **cotyledons** (seed leaves) (*figures 3.14* and *3.15*). **Monocotyledons** have one cotyledon and **dicotyledons** have two. In some seeds, for example shepherd's purse and pea and broad bean,

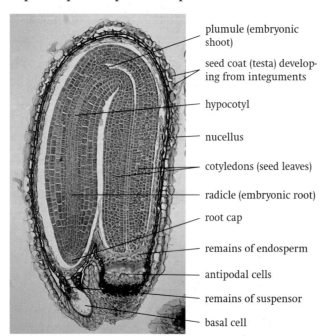

Figure 3.15 LS well-developed embryo of shepherd's purse (*Capsella bursa-pastoris*).

the cotyledons become swollen with nutrients. The nutrients required may be supplied by the endosperm, the nucellus and the parent plant by way of the vascular tissue in the funicle. At germination (page 48) the embryo starts to grow into a new plant (see *box 3.2*).

5 The **micropyle** remains as a tiny pore in the testa through which oxygen and water can later reach the seed when it germinates.

6 As the seed matures, the water content drops markedly from about 90% by mass to about 10–15% by mass. This is in preparation for seed **dormancy** when metabolic activity will be much reduced (chapter 5). Dry seeds respire extremely slowly and can survive extended drought or cold periods.

7 Remaining flower parts, such as the petals and sepals, wither and die and are shed. This is done in a controlled way, similar to the shedding of leaves in the autumn (see *Biology 2*, chapter 6).

Box 3.2
Experiment to investigate embryo development

Embryo development can be studied in a common plant of waste ground and gardens, shepherd's purse (*Capsella bursa-pastoris*), so named because the heart-shaped fruits resemble the purses that were once used by shepherds. The best plants to use are those with small white flowers at the apex and a range of sizes of fruits (the youngest are nearest the apex). The ovules can be dissected out of one of the fruits under a microscope or tripod lens and placed in 5% sodium or potassium hydroxide solution for a few minutes. Individual ovules can then be transferred into two drops of 5% glycerine on a clean microscope slide and covered with a coverslip. When the coverslip is tapped with the handle of a mounted needle, the ovule bursts, and the embryo is exposed. By extracting embryos from a range of fruit sizes, the various stages of embryo development can be followed.

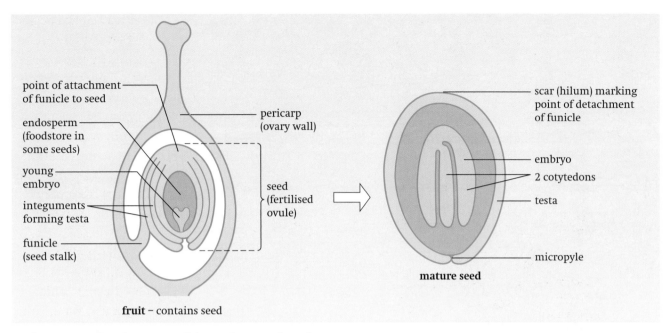

● **Figure 3.16** Development of the embryo and seed.

8 Eventually, seeds are released from the ovary. When the seed breaks off the funicle, a scar is left on the testa called the **hilum**.

SAQ 3.6

Suggest how the structure of cells in the seed may change significantly during preparation for dormancy.

SAQ 3.7

Triploid cells are able to divide by mitosis, but rarely achieve successful meiotic division. Explain why this is so and explain its relevance to the endosperm nucleus.

Development of the fruit

While the seed, or seeds, are developing, other changes take place that result in the development of the **fruit**. Just as the ovule becomes the seed immediately after fertilisation, so the ovary becomes the fruit. Thus

> a fruit is a fertilised ovary.

Table 3.1 summarises some of the changes in the ovary associated with fertilisation and its becoming a fruit. The fruit wall grows and develops from the original ovary wall and is known as the **pericarp**. The fruit contains the seed or seeds and the pericarp is commonly modified to aid their dispersal, for example by becoming fleshy, winged or hard and dry. Examples of fruits with fleshy pericarps, which are attractive to animals, include the tomato, gooseberry, marrow and banana. The oak has a fruit called an acorn with a woody pericarp. This is typical of nuts. Some pericarps form wings to aid dispersal by the wind, as in sycamore, ash and elm. Some pericarps form pods which split along two sides, sometimes twisting to force seeds out violently, e.g. gorse, broom, pea, laburnum and runner bean. Other types of modification also occur.

Before fertilisation	After fertilisation
ovary	fruit
ovary wall	pericarp
ovule	seed
integuments	testa
female gamete and first male gamete	diploid zygote, which grows and develops into the embryo with a plumule (first shoot), radicle (first root) and 1 or 2 cotyledons ('seed leaves')
diploid nucleus and second male gamete	triploid endosperm nucleus, which develops into the endosperm

● **Table 3.1** Summary of changes in the ovary after fertilisation.

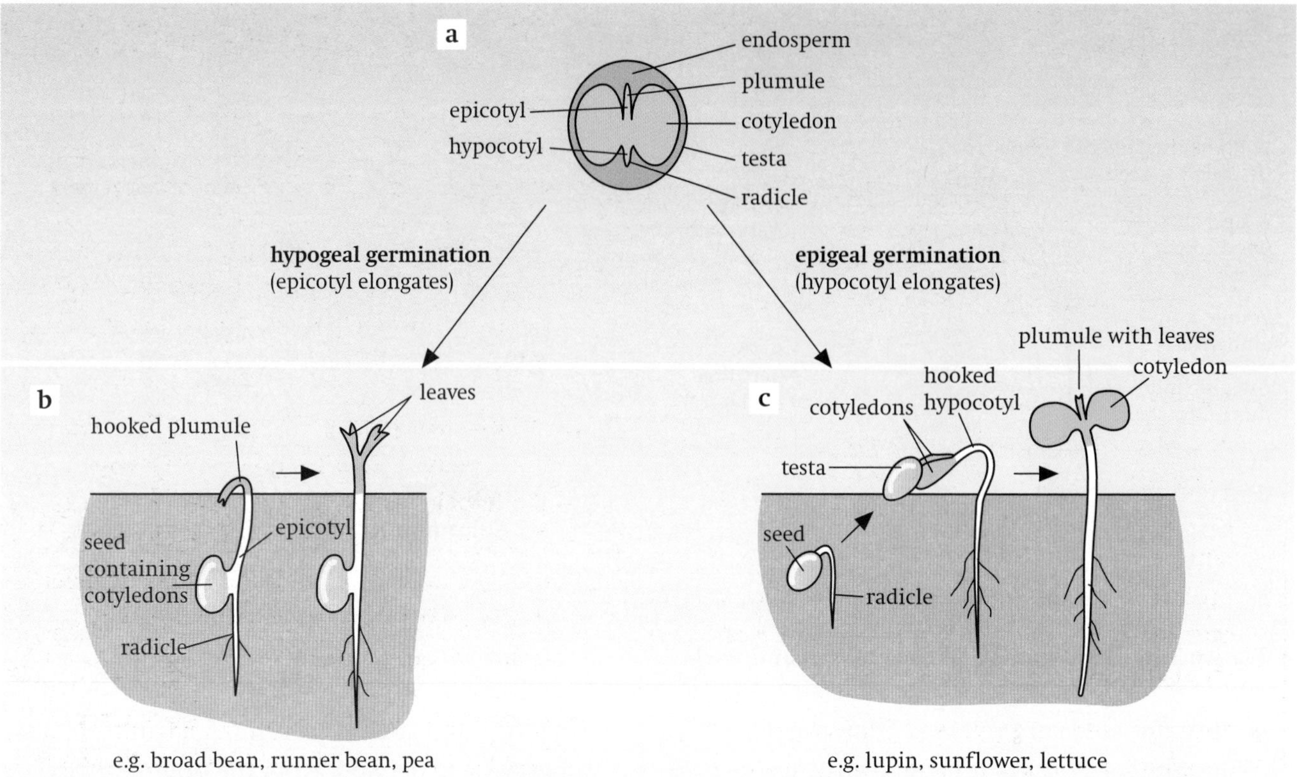

● **Figure 3.17 a** Simplified diagram of a dicotyledonous seed.
b Hypogeal germination. **c** Epigeal germination.

Germination

In dicotyledons there are two types of germination, hypogeal and epigeal (from *hypo*, 'below', *epi*, 'above' and *ge*, 'earth' or 'ground'). In **hypogeal germination** the cotyledons remain in the seed below ground because the first shoot, the plumule, grows from a region just above the cotyledons, called the **epicotyl** ('above cotyledons'). The plumule remains hooked to protect the growing tip as it grows through the soil. In the case of **epigeal germination**, the cotyledons are carried above ground (*figure 3.17*) because growth occurs from the region just below the cotyledons. This region is called the **hypocotyl** and it remains hooked as it grows through the soil. Thus the cotyledons, still enclosed in the testa, are carried up through the soil and become the first photosynthetic structures above the soil. Shepherd's purse shows epigeal germination but other non-endospermous examples that are easier

to see are: broad bean, runner bean, pea (hypogeal) and lupin and sunflower (epigeal). The castor oil seed is an endospermous seed with epigeal germination.

As the hook of the plumule or hypocotyl emerges from the soil, a phytochrome-controlled response to light (see chapter 5) results in the straightening of the hook, and the greening and expansion of the cotyledons (the first leaves). Photosynthesis can then begin and the plant can make its own organic food instead of relying on the food store of the seed. You may wish to look again at SAQ 1.9 and the accompanying text on page 11 to remind yourself about the changes that occur as the plant germinates. Seed dormancy, the role of plant growth regulators during germination, and the physiology of germination are discussed in chapter 5.

SUMMARY

◆ Sexual reproduction is the production of a new organism or organisms involving the production of two haploid gametes and their fusion to form a diploid zygote. Meiosis must occur at some point in the life cycle, so gametes show genetic variation.

◆ The organs of sexual reproduction are produced in flowers in the flowering plants. In the male part of the flower, pollen grains are produced inside pollen sacs. In the female part of the flower, one embryo sac is produced inside each ovule. Meiosis occurs during the formation of pollen grains and embryo sacs.

◆ Two male gametes develop inside each pollen grain. One female gamete and one diploid nucleus develop inside each embryo sac.

◆ Before fertilisation can occur, pollen must be transferred to the female parts of the flower from the male parts, a process called pollination. Self-pollination or cross-pollination occurs. Both have their own particular advantages, and many plants have evolved special mechanisms to promote one or the other.

◆ Cross-pollination produces more genetic variation because two parents are involved. Wind- and insect-pollination particularly favour cross-pollination.

◆ Self-pollination is more reliable and less wasteful of pollen but, as only one parent is involved, inbreeding occurs, restricting genetic variation.

◆ To achieve fertilisation a pollen tube carrying the two male gametes must grow to the ovule.

◆ In flowering plants a double fertilisation takes place. One male gamete fuses with the female gamete to produce the zygote. This develops into the embryo. The other male gamete fuses with the diploid nucleus in the embryo sac to generate a triploid tissue, the endosperm.

◆ In endospermous seeds, the endosperm becomes the food store. In non-endospermous seeds, the endosperm does not develop and the cotyledon or cotyledons (leaves of the embryo) swell with food to become the food store.

◆ The fertilised ovule is the seed. There may be one or more seeds. They are enclosed in the ovary, which is known as the fruit after fertilisation.

◆ At germination, the cotyledons remain below ground (hypogeal germination) or are carried above ground (epigeal germination).

Questions

1 Discuss how the structure of flowers is linked to their function.

2 Discuss the relative merits of self- and cross-pollination.

3 a What is a seed?
  b Describe the structure of a named dicotyledonous seed just before germination and the functions of its various parts.
  c Briefly describe the origins of each of these parts.

Sexual reproduction in humans

By the end of this chapter you should be able to:

1 identify and name the parts of the female and male urinogenital systems;

2 recognise and describe the microscopic structure of the ovary and testis;

3 describe and explain gametogenesis;

4 describe the structures of egg and sperm;

5 explain hormonal control of spermatogenesis;

6 describe and explain the menstrual cycle and hormonal control of oogenesis;

7 describe the passage of sperm from the testes to the oviduct during sexual intercourse;

8 state where and describe how fertilisation occurs;

9 discuss contraception, abortion and *in vitro* fertilisation from biological and ethical viewpoints;

10 describe the structure of the placenta;

11 describe the transport mechanisms involved in placental transfer;

12 describe and explain the functions of the placenta;

13 describe the functions of the amnion;

14 discuss the effects of the actions of the mother on fetal development.

For we humans, as for other animals, the drive to reproduce is one of the most basic and important that there is. We are typical mammals: the fetus develops inside the mother, nourished by the placenta, and has an extended period of development. In this chapter and in part of chapter 5 we will consider some of the biological facts of reproduction in humans, particularly the important role of hormones. But we will also explore some of the important social issues associated with reproduction. Our ability to 'interfere' with or intervene in the process is unique to our species and is increasing all the time. Many important moral, ethical, legal and social issues are raised as a result. Although biologists and the medical profession cannot be expected to have all the answers to the questions raised, they are essential contributors to the inevitable debate within society.

Before we consider exactly how sexual reproduction occurs in humans, it will be helpful to look at the physical structures involved. In both males and females, the urinary system is very closely linked with the reproductive system; this is especially so in the male. Traditionally, therefore, the two systems are studied together as the **urinogenital system (UG system)** as shown by the diagrams in this book. (The urinary system alone is described in *Biology 2*, chapter 6.)

The female reproductive system

Figures 4.1 and *4.2* give a realistic impression of the structure of the human female UG system. *Figure 4.3* is a simplified diagram. Inside the body there are two almond-shaped **ovaries**, about 2.5–5 cm long and 1.5–3 cm wide. They are the origin of the female gametes, the eggs, and they also produce the female sex hormones oestrogen and progesterone. The **oviducts** (also called the **fallopian tubes**) end in funnels fringed with feathery processes called **fimbriae**. They collect secondary oocytes released by the ovaries. Their lining is ciliated and muscular, and the movements of the cilia and muscles sweep the egg towards the uterus (you may remember this from *Biology 1*, chapter 1). Fertilisation takes place in one of the oviducts. The **uterus** is about 7.5 cm long and 5 cm wide (about the size and shape of an inverted pear), but it can grow three to six times larger during pregnancy. It lies behind the bladder and has a thick muscular outer wall (the **myometrium**) and a lining rich in blood vessels (the **endometrium**), which is shed during menstruation. The **cervix** (neck) is the narrow junction between the uterus and the vagina. The ring of muscle in the cervix can close off the uterus and often contains a plug of mucus.

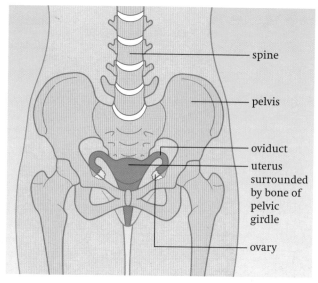

● **Figure 4.2** The pelvic cavity in the female. The pelvis forms a circle of bone which protects the reproductive organs and is large enough to accommodate the uterus during pregnancy.

The **vagina** is a muscular tube about 8–10 cm long running from the base of the uterus to the outside of the body. It is the site where semen is deposited from the penis during sexual intercourse and also the birth canal during childbirth. As well as muscle, the walls contain elastic tissue and the lining (epithelium) is folded. It can therefore enlarge to allow the entry of an erect penis or the exit of a baby. The epithelium of the vagina

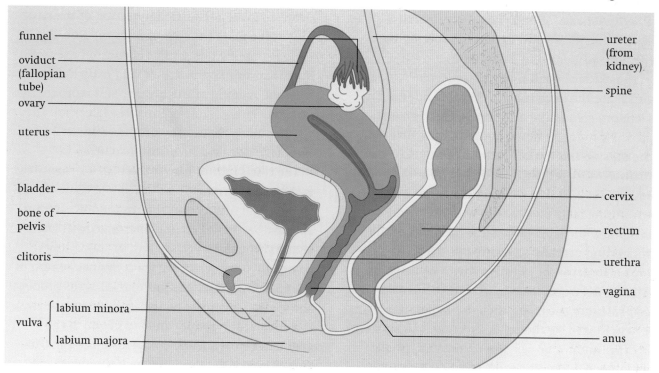

● **Figure 4.1** Side view of female urinogenital system (in section).

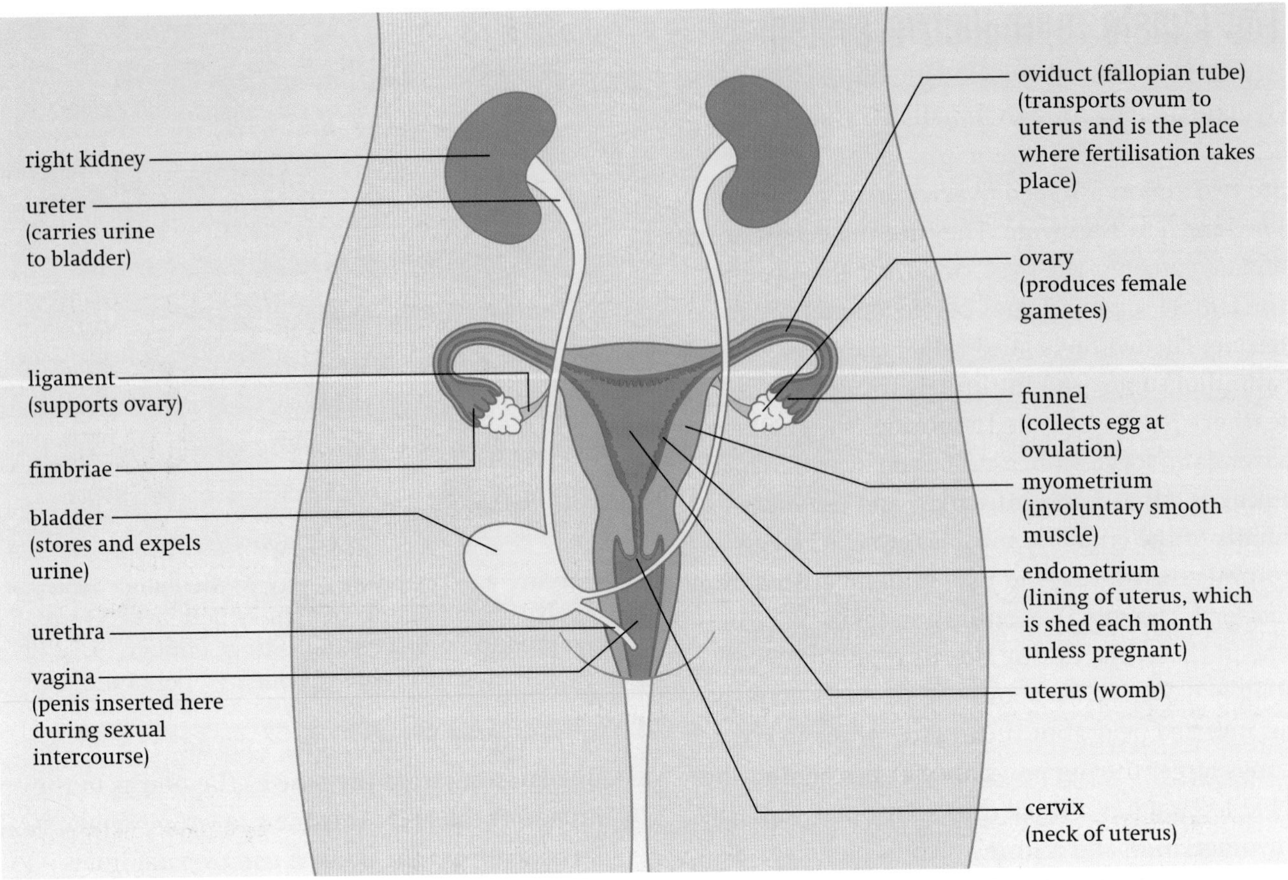

right kidney

ureter
(carries urine
to bladder)

ligament
(supports ovary)

fimbriae

bladder
(stores and expels
urine)

urethra

vagina
(penis inserted here
during sexual
intercourse)

oviduct (fallopian tube)
(transports ovum to
uterus and is the place
where fertilisation takes
place)

ovary
(produces female
gametes)

funnel
(collects egg at
ovulation)

myometrium
(involuntary smooth
muscle)

endometrium
(lining of uterus, which
is shed each month
unless pregnant)

uterus (womb)

cervix
(neck of uterus)

● **Figure 4.3** Female urinogenital system. The bladder is shown moved to one side to reveal the uterus. Note that the urinary and reproductive systems have completely separate openings.

continually secretes a fluid containing mucus, which has an acidic pH (pH 5.7) that deters the growth of harmful microorganisms. Acidic environments are also harmful to sperm, hence the need for semen to be alkaline.

The external genital organs (collectively the **vulva**) are the labia majora, the labia minora, secretory glands and the clitoris. The **labia majora** are the two longitudinal folds of skin visible from the outside and contain fat, smooth muscle and many sensory receptors. The **labia minora** are two smaller folds of skin lying between and mainly within the labia majora, also with many sensory receptors. The labia protect the openings of the vagina and urethra. The **clitoris** is situated at the top (or front) of the vulva, just within the point where the labia minora meet. It is the female equivalent of the penis, though smaller (less than 2.5 cm long). Like the penis, it contains many nerve endings and, when sexually stimulated, swells with blood, becoming erect. It can be a major source of sexual arousal during sexual intercourse.

The male reproductive system

Figure 4.4 gives a realistic impression of the structure of the male UG system from the side. *Figure 4.5* is a simplified diagram drawn from the front. Note that, unlike the female, the male has a *shared* external opening of the urinary and reproductive systems. Both vasa deferentia (see later) and the bladder all open into the urethra, which can therefore carry either urine or semen.

The **testis** (plural **testes**; there are normally two) is the site of production of the male gametes, the **sperm**. (The full technical term for one sperm is **spermatozoan**, and many, **spermatozoa**.) The **seminiferous tubules** are tightly coiled tubes (about 1000 per testis) with a combined length of about 225 metres. Cells lining their walls produce the sperm. The **epididymis** (again, there are two) is a coiled tube about 6 m long in which the sperm are stored while completing their maturation. Some of the fluid in which the sperm are bathed is reabsorbed, making the sperm more

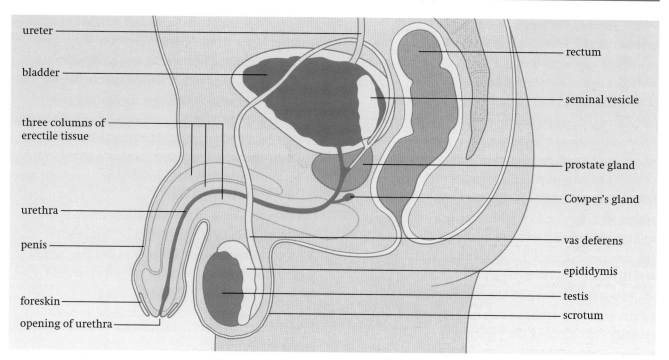

● **Figure 4.4** Side view of male urinogenital system (in section).

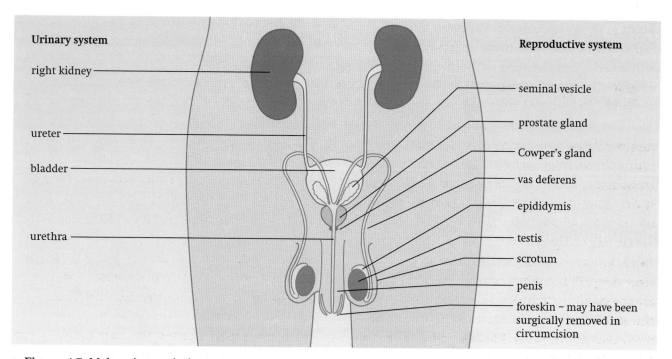

● **Figure 4.5** Male urinogenital system.

concentrated (about 5000 million sperm per cm³).
It is also where the sperm become mobile. The
scrotal sac, or **scrotum**, is a sac of skin containing
the two testes which, unlike the ovaries in the
female, hangs from the main body cavity thus
helping to keep the sperm about 3 °C cooler than
normal body temperature. This is important for
their survival. The **vas deferens** (plural **vasa

deferentia**; there are two of them) is a tube which
carries the sperm out of the testis to the **urethra**.
Sperm are also stored there.

The **prostate gland** (single), **Cowper's glands**
(paired) and **seminal vesicles** (paired) are all
glands which secrete fluid for carrying the sperm
and in which the sperm can swim. Fluid plus
sperm is called **semen**. It has a pH of 7.5.

The fluid of the seminal vesicles is called **seminal fluid**. It is alkaline and neutralises the acidity of any remaining urine in the urethra, as well as helping to neutralise acidity in the vagina. It also contains fructose (a sugar) and sorbitol (similar to a sugar), which are used by the sperm for energy. Other chemicals, with a range of functions, are found. For example, prostaglandins are thought to stimulate muscular activity in the female reproductive tract, aiding the passage of sperm. White blood cells are also present, helping to destroy any bacteria encountered. The fluid of the Cowper's glands is also alkaline and, like seminal fluid, helps to neutralise acidity in the urethra and the vagina. The prostate gland secretes mucus. Like the seminal vesicles, the Cowper's glands and the prostate gland also secrete a range of other chemicals, some of which are probably needed to activate the sperm.

The penis contains the **urethra**, which carries sperm to the outside world. The penis also contains special spongy tissue which can fill with blood when the male is sexually stimulated, causing it to enlarge and become erect and rigid. The penis ejaculates semen into the vagina of the female during sexual intercourse (see page 62).

Gametogenesis

We shall now examine the three main stages of reproduction, namely gametogenesis, fertilisation and development of the zygote. **Gametogenesis** is the formation of gametes. It takes place in the **gonads**, that is the testes in the male and the ovaries in the female. It involves meiosis in the nuclei of diploid 'mother cells' to form haploid gametes. The importance of halving the chromosome number in this way was stressed in *Biology 1* on page 83 and in the previous chapter of this book. It means that when a male gamete

fuses with a female gamete, the normal diploid number is restored. Meiosis also has the important consequence of increasing genetic variation.

Formation of sperm is called **spermatogenesis**. Formation of eggs is called **oogenesis**. The two processes are in essence similar and are shown in *figure 4.6*. In each case, cells of the **germinal epithelium**, which is the outer layer of the ovary or seminiferous tubule, multiply to form **oogonia** in the ovary or **spermatogonia** in the seminiferous tubule. These grow and mature into egg or sperm mother cells, respectively. Egg mother cells are known as **oocytes** and sperm mother cells as **spermatocytes**. The mother cells then divide by meiosis to produce haploid gametes.

SAQ 4.1

Using the information provided in *figure 4.6*,

a how many sperm can be formed from
  (i) one primary spermatocyte,
  (ii) one secondary spermatocyte?

b What is the term used for an immature sperm?

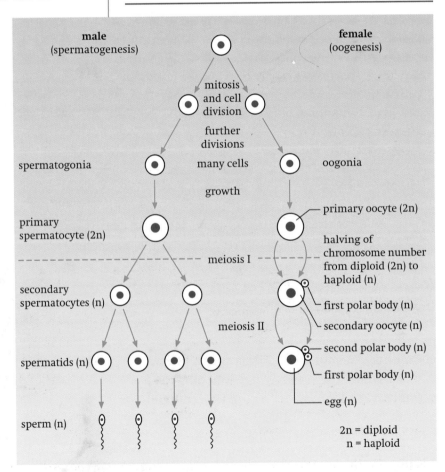

● **Figure 4.6** Diagrammatic representation of gametogenesis in the male and female.

Spermatogenesis

Unlike the female, who produces only one egg per month, the sexually mature human male produces vast numbers of gametes in a continuous production line of several thousand per second (over 100 million per day). This process of spermatogenesis takes place in the testes, shown in section in *figures 4.7 and 4.8*. As we have seen, each testis contains a mass of tiny tubes called the seminiferous tubules and it is in the germinal epithelium of their walls that spermatogenesis takes place (summarised in *figure 4.6*). Sperm development takes place from the outer part of the tube towards the central space of the tube (the lumen) where newly mature sperm break away from the wall and float down the tube towards the epididymis for storage. A ring of special 'nurse' cells, the **Sertoli cells**, is present in the wall. They secrete the fluid found in the lumen of the tubes. All stages of sperm development take place in close association with the Sertoli cells (*figure 4.7b*) and the complex modelling of the cells making up the sperm, particularly the spermatids, is done with their assistance.

Between the tubes are connective tissue, blood vessels and special **interstitial cells**, also known as **cells of Leydig** (*figures 4.7a and 4.8*), which secrete the male sex hormones, including **testosterone**. These hormones circulate in the blood and are important in the development of the male secondary sexual characteristics (that is, those that develop at puberty, see page 95). Testosterone also enters the seminiferous tubules and stimulates the cells that are involved in spermatogenesis, especially the Sertoli cells.

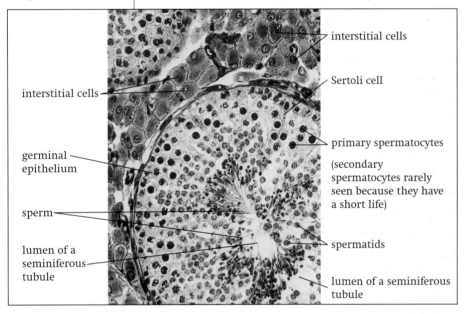

● **Figure 4.8** Transverse section of a testis showing seminiferous tubules with interstitial cells between them (×250). Spermatogonia are visible in the outermost layers of the epithelium lining. Sperm tails are visible at the centre of the main tubule.

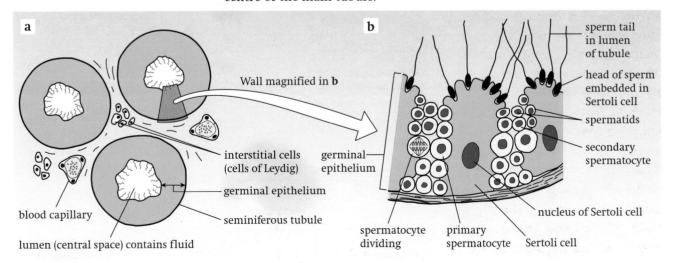

● **Figure 4.7** Diagram showing the microscopic structure of the testis.
a Group of three seminiferous tubules.
b Enlarged portion of the wall of a seminiferous tubule showing stages in sperm development.

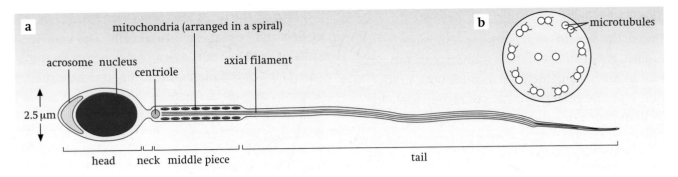

● Figure 4.9
a Structure of a human sperm. Total length is 60 μm.
b TS of tail showing the '9 + 2' arrangement of microtubules.

Structure of the sperm

The structure of a sperm is beautifully linked with its function, as shown in *figure 4.9a*. The **acrosome** is a large, modified lysosome containing the hydrolytic enzymes needed to digest a path to the egg at fertilisation. The **nucleus** carries a haploid set of chromosomes, the genetic information from the male parent. The **axial filament,** which runs all the way from the neck to the tail, is made of microtubules and is responsible for the wave-like beating of the tail which propels it through its fluid surroundings at an average rate of 30 cm per hour. The microtubules have a '9 + 2' arrangement characteristic of flagella and cilia consisting of a ring of nine pairs of microtubules surrounding two central microtubules (*figure 4.9b*). They arise from the **centriole**. The **middle piece** and **tail** are concerned with propulsion. Numerous mitochondria arranged in a spiral within the middle piece provide the energy for beating the tail. This energy is contained in ATP made during aerobic respiration.

Oogenesis

A diagram of a section through a human ovary is shown in *figure 4.10*. *Figure 4.11* shows the structure of a rabbit ovary as seen in section with a light microscope. Unlike the situation in the

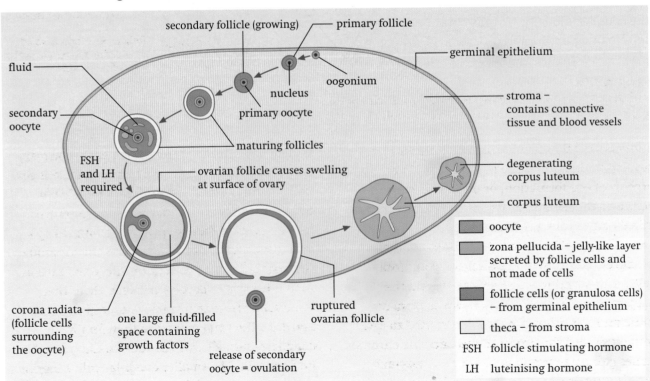

● Figure 4.10 Stages in the development of one follicle in a human ovary. Arrows show sequence of events.

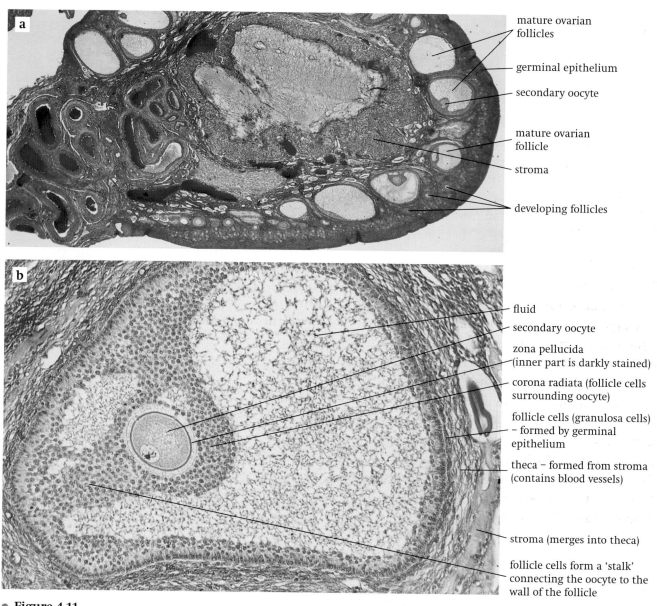

mature ovarian follicles

germinal epithelium

secondary oocyte

mature ovarian follicle

stroma

developing follicles

fluid

secondary oocyte

zona pellucida (inner part is darkly stained)

corona radiata (follicle cells surrounding oocyte)

follicle cells (granulosa cells) – formed by germinal epithelium

theca – formed from stroma (contains blood vessels)

stroma (merges into theca)

follicle cells form a 'stalk' connecting the oocyte to the wall of the follicle

● **Figure 4.11**
a LS ovary of a rabbit showing developing follicles (× 16).
b High power detail of one mature ovarian follicle (× 100).

human, several ovarian (Graafian) follicles may develop at the same time in the rabbit. The process of egg formation, or oogenesis, starts before birth. The outer layer of the ovary, the germinal epithelium, produces many oogonia that grow to form **primary oocytes** (*figure 4.6*). It also produces cells known as **follicle** or **granulosa** cells, which multiply and cluster around the oocytes, forming structures known as **primary follicles**. Each primary oocyte has started to divide by meiosis, but the process stops once the chromosomes pair up in prophase I. They are suspended in this state for years – some for a lifetime. By the time a baby is born, about two million primary

follicles are already present, each with a primary oocyte in prophase I. Once a human female is sexually mature, usually one primary follicle per month is stimulated to complete development into an **ovarian follicle**. This is surrounded by a layer called the **theca** that secretes the hormone **oestrogen**. The follicle cells multiply and several fluid-filled spaces develop between them that eventually merge to form one space (*figures 4.10 and 4.11*). The primary oocyte then finally completes meiosis I and divides *unequally* into two haploid cells. The smaller daughter cell is known as a **polar body** and, in humans, eventually disintegrates. The larger daughter cell is known as the

secondary oocyte and this, together with some of the surrounding follicle cells, is the ovarian follicle. The ovarian follicle is large enough (about 1 cm in diameter) to cause a blister-like swelling on the surface of the ovary when fully mature (*figure 4.10*) that can be seen using a laparoscope (see page 79). At this stage, the secondary oocyte is released into the oviduct, a process known as **ovulation**. If it is fertilised, it completes meiosis II as described later. It is only then that, strictly speaking, it can be called an ovum or egg. Until then it has been suspended at metaphase II. After ovulation the empty follicle develops into a **corpus luteum** (yellow body), which gradually degenerates unless fertilisation takes place. The corpus luteum secretes the hormone **progesterone**.

Structure of the secondary oocyte and egg

The structure of the secondary oocyte and egg is shown in *figure 4.12*. The egg is the largest cell in the human body (140 μm or 0.14 mm in diameter) and is just visible with the naked eye. Unlike the eggs of many animals it contains no conspicuous yolk, although it does have a lipid food reserve. It also obtains nutrients from the surrounding follicle cells. The lysosomes contain enzymes and have a role at fertilisation (page 63).

SAQ 4.2
List the main differences between a human sperm and egg, giving brief reasons for the differences. What important similarity do they have?

Hormonal control of gametogenesis

There are certain important similarities between the hormonal control of spermatogenesis and oogenesis. In both cases the control centres are the **hypothalamus** and the **pituitary gland**. Also in both cases, the pituitary gland secretes two gonadotrophic hormones: **follicle stimulating hormone (FSH)** and **luteinising hormone (LH)**. (The term gonadotrophic means that they stimulate gonads, that is the testes and ovaries.) The gonadotrophic hormones themselves are secreted in response to a hormone signal from the hypothalamus. This hormone is **gonadotrophin releasing hormone (GnRH)** and is transported in a special blood vessel linking the hypothalamus with the anterior lobe of the pituitary gland. GnRH must be present for normal gonad function, and is also one means by which the central nervous system can influence reproduction. The hypothalamus and pituitary gland act as the controlling link between the nervous system and the endocrine system. (There is more about this in chapter 5, page 92.)

Regulation of gonadotrophins also involves **negative feedback** from hormones produced by the gonads. In order to understand the following detailed accounts, it will be useful to recall the principles of negative feedback by referring to page 88 of *Biology 2*.

Hormonal control of spermatogenesis

The hormonal control of spermatogenesis is summarised in *figure 4.13*. Spermatogenesis is dependent on the production of testosterone by the testes. In turn, production of testosterone is controlled by the pituitary gland. (This can be

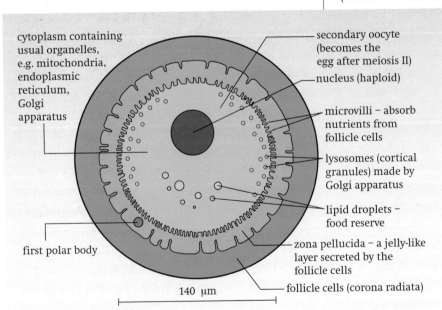

cytoplasm containing usual organelles, e.g. mitochondria, endoplasmic reticulum, Golgi apparatus

first polar body

140 μm

secondary oocyte (becomes the egg after meiosis II)

nucleus (haploid)

microvilli – absorb nutrients from follicle cells

lysosomes (cortical granules) made by Golgi apparatus

lipid droplets – food reserve

zona pellucida – a jelly-like layer secreted by the follicle cells

follicle cells (corona radiata)

● **Figure 4.12** Structure of the secondary oocyte and surrounding structures at ovulation. At fertilisation, the secondary oocyte divides (meiosis II) to form the egg and a second polar body. The egg has the same structure as the secondary oocyte, but there is one more polar body after meiosis II.

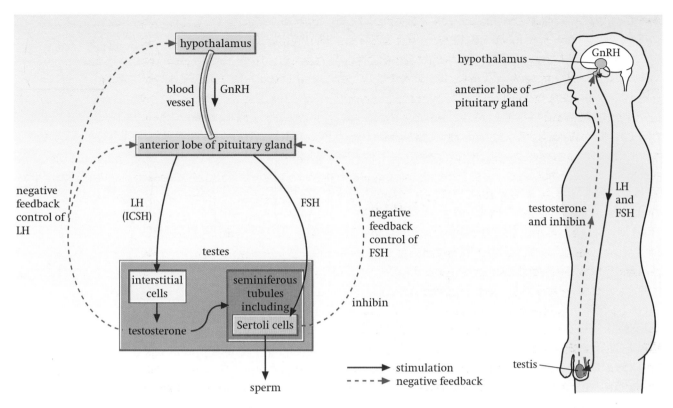

● **Figure 4.13** Summary of hormonal control of spermatogenesis. Seminiferous
tubules, including Sertoli cells, must be active for successful production of sperm.
In the male, hormone production is continuous, not cyclic as in the female.

deduced from the observation that if the pituitary
gland is removed from a rat, its testes shrink in size,
spermatogenesis ceases and testosterone levels
decline. If doses of testosterone are then given to
the rat, the changes can be partly reversed.) The
anterior lobe of the pituitary gland achieves this
control by secreting LH. As mentioned, this hormone is secreted by both male and female. In the
male it has an alternative name, **interstitial cell
stimulating hormone (ICSH)** although LH is pre-
ferred. It travels in the blood from the pituitary to
its targets, which are specific receptors on the membranes of the interstitial cells of the testes. Here it
stimulates the production of testosterone from the
steroid, cholesterol. Testosterone then stimulates
spermatogenesis in the seminiferous tubules.

For completely normal levels of sperm
production, another pituitary hormone, FSH, is also
needed. FSH binds to specific receptors on the
membranes of Sertoli cells and makes them much
more active, stimulating sperm development and
the secretion of fluid into the seminiferous tubules.
Regulation of LH is brought about by testosterone in
a process of negative feedback as follows. An

increase in the level of testosterone results in a
decrease in GnRH production by the hypothalamus
which in turn reduces the levels of LH and FSH produced by the anterior pituitary gland. Testosterone
also acts directly on the pituitary gland to reduce
LH secretion. Further regulation of FSH is thought
to be achieved by a product of the Sertoli cells
known as **inhibin,** which is released if spermatogenesis is too rapid, targetting the pituitary gland.

The menstrual cycle and hormonal control of oogenesis

Figure 4.14 summarises the hormonal control of
the menstrual cycle. As we have seen, the gametes
and sex hormones in the male are produced continuously but, in the female, events are cyclic: on
average every 28 days. There are two halves to the
cycle. In the first half, an egg (or more correctly a
secondary oocyte) is produced; in the second half,
the uterus is prepared for implantation in case
the egg is fertilised. The complete cycle involves
the ovaries, the uterus, the pituitary gland and
the hypothalamus and, in humans, is known as
the **menstrual cycle** ('menstrual' means monthly).
The first day of the cycle is by convention counted

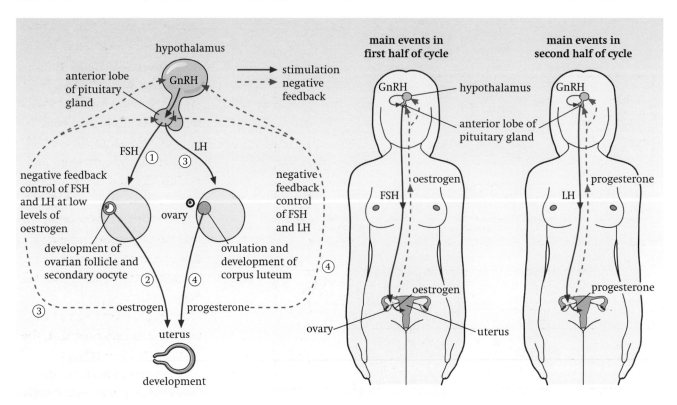

● **Figure 4.14** Summary of hormonal control of the menstrual cycle. Note both oestrogen and progesterone have a negative feedback effect on the hypothalamus as well as the anterior pituitary gland.

from the start of **menstruation** (a 'period'). This is the shedding of the endometrium (the bloody lining of the uterus) through the vagina that occurs if fertilisation has *not* taken place.

The sequence of events is summarised as follows.

1 In response to GnRH from the hypothalamus, the anterior lobe of the pituitary gland secretes FSH into the blood. Its target is the ovary, where it stimulates development of a primary follicle.

2 The follicle secretes low levels of oestrogen into the blood, gradually increasing in amount as the follicle grows. Oestrogen has three main targets, the uterus, the anterior lobe of the pituitary gland and the hypothalamus. In the uterus it stimulates repair and, later, thickening of the endometrium. This involves the development of more blood vessels and glands. In the anterior lobe of the pituitary, low levels of oestrogen inhibit secretion of FSH and LH, another example of negative feedback. In the hypothalamus, oestrogen is responsible for negative feedback inhibition of GnRH. *Figure 4.15* shows how the production of oestrogen increases as the follicle grows, and the relatively high levels just before ovulation. When levels of oestrogen increase

greatly over a time span of at least two days, LH and FSH secretion is *stimulated* rather than inhibited. Thus oestrogen has a double role in the pituitary and hypothalamus. The whole process is very finely tuned.

3 In response to GnRH, LH and FSH are produced in a 'surge' at around day 14 of the cycle, i.e. a relatively large amount in a relatively short time. The target of LH is the ovary. It causes **ovulation**, which is defined as the release of the secondary oocyte from the ovarian follicle. The surge ensures the precise timing of ovulation, which usually occurs within 24 hours of the surge and, on average, 14 days into the cycle (*figure 4.15*). LH also stimulates the remains of the ovarian follicle to develop into the corpus luteum, stimulates the corpus luteum to secrete another hormone, progesterone, and *reduces* oestrogen production. The return to low levels of oestrogen now reduces FSH and LH secretion, by negative feedback.

4 The corpus luteum secretes both oestrogen and progesterone. Progesterone has three targets, the uterus, the anterior lobe of the pituitary gland and the hypothalamus. In the uterus it

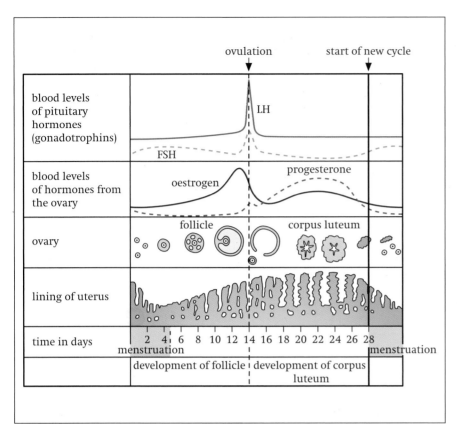

● **Figure 4.15** Summary of changes during the menstrual cycle.

stimulates glandular activity in the endometrium, and helps oestrogen in maintaining its thickness. In the pituitary and hypothalamus, high levels of progesterone enhance the negative feedback effects of oestrogen and inhibit FSH and LH secretion from the pituitary and GnRH from the hypothalamus. Release of progesterone is associated with a small temperature rise in the female body (*figure 4.16*).

5 If the egg is fertilised and the woman becomes pregnant, the corpus luteum receives a hormone stimulus from the implanted embryo, but if such a stimulus is *not* received, no fertilisation having taken place, the corpus luteum starts to

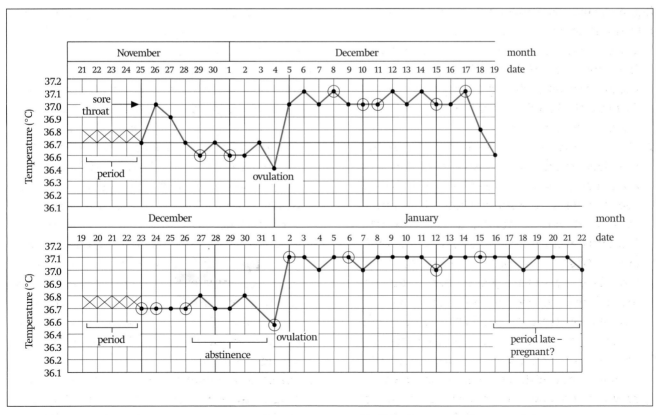

● **Figure 4.16** Temperature chart for a woman who was receiving fertility advice and trying to get pregnant. Occasions when sexual intercourse took place are circled.

degenerate. The reason for this is uncertain, but is probably due to a chemical produced by the corpus luteum itself. (Pharmaceutical companies are interested in this possibility because such a chemical might be useful as a medical drug to induce early abortions.) As the corpus luteum degenerates, the supply of oestrogen and progesterone is of course cut off. FSH is no longer inhibited and is therefore switched on and stimulates the formation of a new primary follicle, thus completing the cycle. The lining of the uterus breaks down at this stage, causing menstruation (a period). This typically continues for about the first five days of the next cycle (figure 4.15).

SAQ 4.3

Study figure 4.16.
a Suggest why it is important to take the temperature at the same time every day.
b Why would the woman be advised to record any illness, such as a sore throat, on the chart?
c What is the normal temperature (i) before ovulation, (ii) after ovulation?
d What effect does pregnancy have on temperature?
e On what date(s) is she most likely to have conceived?

SAQ 4.4

Blood plasma concentrations of FSH and LH increase markedly if the ovaries are removed or after menopause (page 95). Suggest a reason.

Passage of sperm from testes to oviduct

We have looked at the production of oocyte and sperm. Now, for fertilisation to take place, they must meet. Sperm must travel from the seminiferous tubules in the male, where they are made, to the oviduct in the female.

Transport in the male

The seminiferous tubules of the testes are grouped into bundles of about 100. From each bundle one tube emerges, connecting the bundle to the epididymis. Each sperm spends about six to 12 days moving with the fluid from the seminiferous tubule and through the epididymis. Chemical changes in the fluid activate the sperm and they become motile. They are moved by muscular activity of the walls of the tubes from the epididymis into the vas deferens. At this stage they would already be capable of fertilising an egg, but more fluid is added from the seminal vesicles, prostate and Cowper's glands (see page 53) to form semen, the mixture of sperm and seminal fluid. (The combined fluids probably increase fertility.)

Sexual intercourse

The sperm are introduced into the female during sexual intercourse (also called coitus, copulation or just sex). The fascinating related topics of social interaction, courtship and sexual behaviour are outside the scope of this book, and much of the biology of sexual behaviour is still poorly understood. For example, the effects of stress, social interaction and other environmental factors on fertility are important but, until recently, relatively neglected areas of research. Here we will consider just the physical and chemical processes involved.

Sexual excitement of the male, either psychological or physical, results in erection of the penis. Erection is caused by dilation of arteries entering the penis and the flow of arterial blood into a special spongy tissue. In addition, the veins leading out of the penis constrict, resulting in raised blood pressure and higher blood volume within the penis. If sexual stimulation continues, it eventually comes to a climax with **orgasm**, when there is contraction of the muscles of the prostate gland, seminal vesicles, vasa deferentia and urethra. This causes ejaculation of the semen. In this way, a total volume of about $3\,cm^3$ of semen, containing on average 150–300 million sperm, can be introduced into the vagina of the female.

During coitus in the female, the blood supply to the sexual organs increases. The labia swell and the clitoris may become erect. The vagina expands and extra mucous fluid is secreted inside it. This can lubricate the action of the penis. If orgasm occurs, there are muscular contractions of both the vagina and uterus.

Transport in the female

By sexual intercourse, the sperm are deposited at the top of the vagina near the cervix. They can survive for one to two days in the female. The alkaline semen helps to protect them from the acid fluid (pH 5.7) of the vagina. Most of the sperm are thought to leak from the vagina without penetrating the cervix. The cervix is blocked by a plug of mucus. Its consistency changes during the menstrual cycle and it is only thin enough to allow passage of sperm during the first part of the cycle, before progesterone levels become high. It is thought that movement of the sperm through the uterus and into the oviducts does not depend on muscular contractions of the uterus, but partly on the sperm's own swimming and partly on the action of cilia lining the uterus and oviducts (*figure 4.17*). It probably takes at least four to eight hours for living sperm to reach the oviducts.

Capacitation

If freshly ejaculated sperm are mixed with eggs in the laboratory, as they are with *in vitro* fertilisation (the 'test tube baby' technique, see page 79), fertilisation is not possible for several hours. The process which the sperm must first undergo, which gives them the capacity to fertilise an egg, is called **capacitation** and takes about seven hours. It involves the removal of a layer of glycoprotein and plasma proteins from the outer surface of the sperm. Glycoprotein is added by the epididymis, and plasma proteins come from the seminal fluid. They are normally removed by enzymes in the uterus (*figure 4.17*). Their removal probably results in a stronger 'whiplash' beating of the sperm tail, making it swim more rapidly. It also exposes the plasma membrane of the sperm and makes it more sensitive to chemical signals from the secondary oocyte, allowing the acrosome reaction to occur (see below). The plasma membrane also becomes more permeable to calcium ions, which are needed for increased motility and for the acrosome reaction.

Acrosome reaction

Once capacitation has taken place, sperm can finally be activated to achieve fertilisation. This takes place in the oviduct and is triggered by chemicals secreted by the follicle cells, or **zona pellucida**, around the secondary oocyte. It includes a stage known as the **acrosome reaction**, in which the acrosome in the sperm head (*figure 4.9*) swells and its membrane fuses in several places with the plasma membrane surrounding the sperm head. This allows the enzymes inside the acrosome to escape in a process of exocytosis (*figure 4.18*).Calcium ions are needed for the acrosome reaction to occur.

Fertilisation

We have seen that, after ovulation, the secondary oocyte and surrounding cells are swept into the funnel at the end of the oviduct (*figure 4.3*) and along the oviduct by the action of the ciliated lining. After sexual intercourse, the secondary oocyte and its surrounding cells become surrounded by sperm (*figures 4.18 and 4.19*). The processes leading from here to fertilisation are described in *figure 4.18*. Remember that the sperm penetrates a **secondary oocyte**, which is thus stimulated to complete meiosis II. The

● **Figure 4.17** False-colour scanning electron micrograph of human sperm (yellow) in the uterus. The ciliated epithelium of the endometrium is visible (green). (× 4000)

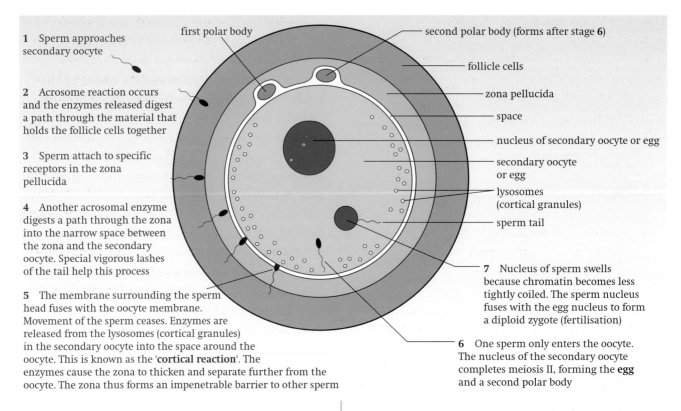

1   Sperm approaches secondary oocyte

2   Acrosome reaction occurs and the enzymes released digest a path through the material that holds the follicle cells together

3   Sperm attach to specific receptors in the zona pellucida

4   Another acrosomal enzyme digests a path through the zona into the narrow space between the zona and the secondary oocyte. Special vigorous lashes of the tail help this process

5   The membrane surrounding the sperm head fuses with the oocyte membrane. Movement of the sperm ceases. Enzymes are released from the lysosomes (cortical granules) in the secondary oocyte into the space around the oocyte. This is known as the 'cortical reaction'. The enzymes cause the zona to thicken and separate further from the oocyte. The zona thus forms an impenetrable barrier to other sperm

first polar body

second polar body (forms after stage **6**)

follicle cells

zona pellucida

space

nucleus of secondary oocyte or egg

secondary oocyte or egg

lysosomes (cortical granules)

sperm tail

7   Nucleus of sperm swells because chromatin becomes less tightly coiled. The sperm nucleus fuses with the egg nucleus to form a diploid zygote (fertilisation)

6   One sperm only enters the oocyte. The nucleus of the secondary oocyte completes meiosis II, forming the **egg** and a second polar body

● **Figure 4.18** Events leading to fertilisation.

cell then divides to form what can now truly be called an **egg** and a second polar body. **Fertilisation** is the fusion of a sperm with the egg to form a single diploid cell, the zygote. It takes place in one of the oviducts. Penetration of the follicle cells surrounding the oocyte is shown in *figure 4.20.*

SAQ 4.5

a   Using *figure 4.18*, describe how penetration of more than one sperm into the secondary oocyte is prevented.

b   Why is it important that only one sperm enters the secondary oocyte?

c   Why are such large numbers of sperm produced if only one is needed for fertilisation?

● **Figure 4.19** Coloured SEM of a sperm approaching a secondary oocyte, just before fertilisation. The oocyte's surface is covered with microvilli.

● **Figure 4.20** False-colour TEM showing penetration of a secondary oocyte by a single sperm, prior to fertilisation. The sperm is in the space between the oocyte and the zona pellucida, and its receptor sites are binding to the oocyte. (× 2900)

Sperm may survive for up to three days in the woman's body, but they gradually lose their ability to fertilise the egg. After fertilisation, the zygote nucleus starts to divide by mitosis, thus beginning the development of the embryo. The first division occurs about 30 hours after intercourse. The embryo is still free in the oviduct until it reaches the uterus, about four days after ovulation, and becomes attached to the uterus wall. This process is called **implantation** and is complete by six days after ovulation. A hormone produced by the embryo, **chorionic gonadotrophin (CG)**, prevents degeneration of the corpus luteum, and is the signal to the ovary that the woman is pregnant.

SAQ 4.6

Why is maintaining the corpus luteum important if pregnancy is to proceed?

A detailed description of the further development of the embryo and, later, the fetus is outside the scope of this book, but development of the placenta and its role in supporting the fetus are covered (pages 67–71). First, we shall examine how pregnancy can be *avoided* by contraception.

Contraception

Humans, and a few of the apes, are the only vertebrates that are sexually active throughout the reproductive cycle. This may be because sexual activity has evolved an additional role, that of 'pair bonding' and reinforcing the emotional relationships between couples. However, for various reasons, it is usual for people, especially in modern societies, to want to limit the number of children they have.

Conception is the beginning of pregnancy and, in the strict sense of the word, **contraception** means 'taking action to avoid conception'. However, there are other procedures generally regarded as contraception that are effective *after* conception and result in the death of embryos. This raises ethical issues for some people. For cultural or religious reasons, some people are opposed to contraception, or 'unnatural' methods of contraception. For instance, 'natural' methods are the only forms of contraception officially allowed by the Roman Catholic Church.

The main forms of contraception, their modes of action and their relative advantages and disadvantages are summarised in *table 4.1*. As the table reveals, there is at present no ideal contraceptive, so there is constant research into better methods. There has, for example, been much research into a *male* equivalent of 'the pill', a hormonal contraceptive pill or injection, which, like the pill used by women, is easy to take, virtually 100% reliable and has minimal side-effects. In 1986, the World Health Organisation funded trials in which men received testosterone injections once a week to inhibit spermatogenesis. Results showed the method was 70–95% effective. A testosterone nasal spray and an implant (a device for slow release into the blood) are now being researched, in parallel with the progesterone trials mentioned in *table 4.1*.

SAQ 4.7

Suggest how testosterone may inhibit spermatogenesis.

SAQ 4.8

Explain how progesterone could act as a male contraceptive.

SAQ 4.9

Suggest reasons why a pharmaceutical company might be **a** reluctant and **b** keen to develop a male pill.

SAQ 4.10

An anti-progesterone contraceptive is being developed for women. From your knowledge of the effects of progesterone before and after conception, what ethical arguments might there be against it?

Ethical issues of contraception

As a species, we are increasingly able to intervene in our own reproduction, for instance by contraception, abortion and *in vitro* fertilisation (see later). Many important ethical issues arise from these examples, some global and some local. Ethics is the study of what is considered 'right'

Method	Mode of action	Effectiveness* if used correctly	Particular advantages	Particular disadvantages
Natural			no physical side-effects.	psychological side-effects possible
• total abstinence	avoid sexual intercourse at all times	100%	totally effective and simple	may restrict emotional development of a relationship
• periodic abstinence	avoid intercourse around ovulation	85–93%	allowed by Roman Catholic Church. When used together, can increase reliability of rhythm method	requires good knowledge of body and record-keeping and a well-negotiated relationship
1 rhythm method	woman uses calendar to chart cycle and avoids intercourse for about 7 days out of 28			relies on regular cycle, high failure rate
2 temperature method	woman monitors her temperature which rises by about 0.6°C at ovulation	about 80%		requires temperature to be taken at the same time each day
3 Billings method	note changes in vaginal secretions around ovulation from thick, cloudy and sticky to thin, clear and stretchy	75–90%		
• withdrawal (coitus interruptus)	man withdraws penis before ejaculation	about 80%	allowed by Roman Catholic Church	low success rate because semen leaks from penis before ejaculation. Frustration if climax not reached. Considerable willpower required
Barrier	block sperm from reaching egg or inactivate sperm chemically			
• condom (sheath)	thin rubber sheath placed over erect penis, preventing escape of sperm into vagina	97% (evidence shows less successful in first year of use)	simple, cheap, quite reliable, easily obtained. Increasingly popular because it also protects against sexually transmitted diseases including HIV	care must be taken to avoid damage to condom and that no spillage of semen occurs on withdrawal. Requires interruption of love-making to fit sheath
• female condom (Femidom)	thin rubber or polyurethane tube, closed at one end. Three times wider than a male condom. Has two flexible rings, one at each end, to keep it in place. Forms a lining to the vagina. The closed end fits inside the vagina and the open end stays outside, flat against the vulva	relatively new, so not much data available. Expected to be same as male condom	as male condom. Can be inserted any time before intercourse, and removed any time later. No odour and does not grip around the penis	partly visible outside body
• cap (diaphragm or Dutch cap)	a soft rubber cap which covers the cervix and prevents entry of sperm. Inserted before intercourse. Caps are of various sizes and design. Used with a spermicide cream which kills sperm. Must be left in place at least six hours after intercourse	85–97%	can be inserted a few hours before intercourse	training required to fit cap. Need to check every six months that cap is right size and correctly fitted. Occasionally causes abdominal pain
• sponge	sponge impregnated with spermicide. Fits over cervix. Disposable. Fit up to 24 hours before intercourse. Leave in place at least six hours after intercourse	75–85%	easier than cap because one size fits all and no fitting required	relatively high failure rate

Method	Mode of action	Effectiveness* if used correctly	Particular advantages	Particular disadvantages
Surgical				
• Male sterilisation – vasectomy	each vas deferens is tied and cut by a surgeon	100%	very reliable. Simple. No side-effects. Semen still produced, but without sperm	very difficult to reverse
• Female sterilisation – tubal ligation	oviducts tied and cut by a surgeon	100%	very reliable	very difficult to reverse. Operation more difficult and possibility of reversal even less than in male
Hormonal	prevent ovulation or spermatogenesis		reliable and convenient	sometimes medical side-effects
• female combined pill	contains oestrogen and progesterone. Pill taken orally daily for 21 or 28 days each month	99–100%	convenient. Does not interfere with love-making. Extremely reliable. Gives regular periods. Reduces period pains	minor side-effects possible. Not suitable for older women or smokers over 35, or those with risk of heart disease or strokes. Serious side-effects possible (though rare). Available only on prescription
• female mini-pill	contains progesterone only. Ovulation may occur, but cervical mucus thickened and prevents entry of sperm	98%	lower dose of hormone and therefore less risk to older women. Can be taken while breast-feeding without affecting quantity or quality of milk	monthly cycle may be irregular, with breakthrough bleeding. Minor side-effects possible, e.g. headaches. Must be taken same time each day (or no more than three hours late)
• male pill	synthetic form of progesterone inhibits production of testosterone and sperm via effect on brain. Testosterone loss is counteracted by six-monthly injection or implant	on trial	does not interfere with love-making. Opportunity for male responsibility	still on trial. Side-effects not yet fully known. Testosterone must be replaced – some side effects on liver function
• injectable	progesterone injected into muscle of woman for long-term, slow release. Stops ovulation. Only recommended if other methods unsuitable	over 99%	one injection protects for up to 12 weeks	periods usually irregular. May delay return to fertility when stopped
Post-fertilisation	prevents implantation			technically involves death of embryo
• intra-uterine device (IUD or coil)	small device, usually plastic with copper, inserted into uterus by doctor and left in place.	96–99%	effective for up to 5 years Particularly suitable for older women. Does not interfere with love-making	periods may be heavier at first. IUD may come out. May lead to pelvic infection. Often causes cramps and pain
• 'morning-after' pill	pill(s) containing high doses of hormone taken within three days of intercourse	high	used in emergency when intercourse has taken place without contraception	long-term effects unknown. Therefore should not be used on a regular basis

* Effectiveness: 75% effectiveness means 25% failure; that is 25 pregnancies per 100 women using the method per year. Unprotected sex results in 90% failure.

● **Table 4.1** Contraception – methods, modes of action and relative advantages and disadvantages.

and 'wrong' by a given group of people. A society's ethics may change with time. It has been said that it is the job of scientists to solve problems. Should scientists then be involved with ethical issues where we sometimes have to accept that there are *no* 'right' solutions, or that what is right for some may be wrong for others? In discussing ethical issues associated with reproduction it can be argued that it is important to be well-informed scientifically. Biological knowledge, combined with the willingness to listen with respect to the views and experience of others, is essential in the debate.

The following are some of the ethical issues associated with contraception.

- The Roman Catholic Church, influential in much of the world, argues that the use of contraception apart from periodic abstinence (*table 4.1*) is interference with a natural process of procreation which should be left to the 'will of God'; the enjoyment of sex is regarded as a gift that should not be separated from the purpose of creation. However, having many children may condemn families to lives of poverty, especially in developing countries.

- Women may resort to abortion, either legal or illegal, as an alternative to contraception (see also the ethical issues associated with abortion on page 77). Is abortion a less acceptable solution than contraception?

- Large families and a high rate of population growth place strains on the resources of societies.

- Should more advice about contraception be given to young people? If so, at what age and by whom should the advice be given?

- Should contraceptives be made more easily available? For example, should schools or colleges have contraceptive vending machines?

- Should methods which prevent implantation be avoided since a potential human life is destroyed?

- Some contraceptives may be associated with long-term health risks, for example the pill and RU486, an anti-progesterone drug which aborts the fetus (see page 77).

- Should research into male contraception be given a higher priority, and should men be encouraged to take more responsibility?

Development of the zygote

We have considered gametogenesis, fertilisation and first division of the zygote. Now we can consider development of the implanted embryo. (Note that, once differentiation of the formerly identical cells of the embryo has occurred and development of the typically human characteristics begun, the embryo is referred to as a **fetus**.)

The placenta

The **placenta** is a structure found only in mammals. In humans, it develops over the first two to three months of pregnancy and is an organ in its own right. It is unique in that it is formed from the tissues of two, genetically different, individuals, the mother and the fetus. Its function is to allow the exchange of materials between mother and fetus.

Structure of the placenta

Figure 4.21 shows the structure of the placenta. Early in development, a layer called the **chorion** develops from the embryo and invades the uterus wall, forming many finger-like projections called **chorionic villi**. These project into blood-filled spaces formed from expansion of the mother's blood vessels. Inside the villi, tree-like networks of fine blood vessels develop from the fetus. Villi and capillaries together provide a large surface area for the exchange of materials with the mother's blood. The epithelial cells of the villi have **microvilli**, increasing the surface area for uptake even more.

Deoxygenated blood from the fetus, carrying waste products such as carbon dioxide and urea, is pumped by the heart of the fetus in two blood vessels to the placenta. These two blood vessels are arteries because they are carrying blood away from the heart even though it is *deoxygenated* blood. The arteries reach the placenta through the **umbilical cord** (*figure 4.22*). In the placenta the arteries branch into the villi where they form capillaries. A fetal vein carries oxygenated blood back to the heart of the fetus through the umbilical cord to be circulated around the body of the fetus. Note that this is an example of a vein carrying *oxygenated* blood.

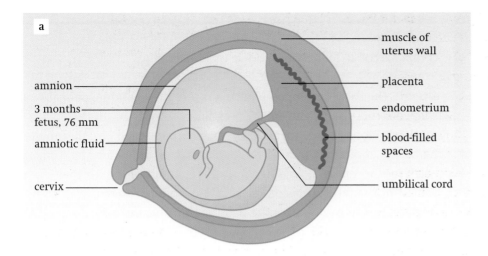

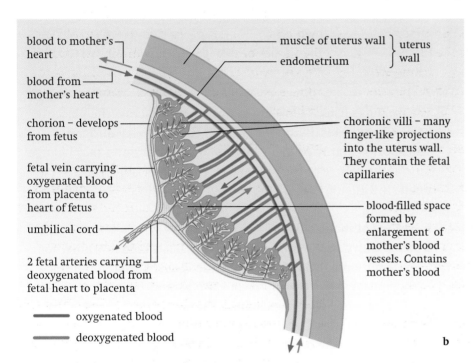

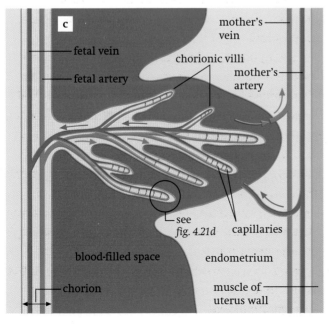

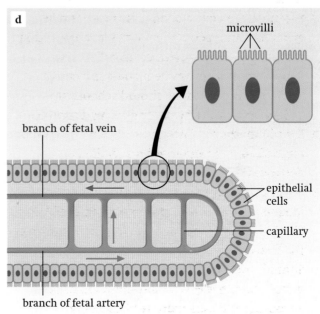

- **Figure 4.21**
  a Diagram showing how the umbilical cord and placenta link the fetus to the mother's blood supply.
  b Diagram of placenta showing chorionic villi and the blood supplies of fetus and mother.
  c Detail of chorionic villi showing capillaries.
  d Detail of blood supply and epithelium of chorionic villus.

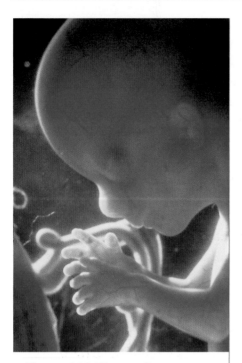

● **Figure 4.22** Human fetus at about 4 months (16 weeks) showing the head and upper limbs and the umbilical cord which connects the fetus to the placenta. The eyelids have not yet fully developed.

As blood circulates through the capillaries in the chorionic villi, useful substances such as nutrients and oxygen cross from the mother's blood spaces into the capillaries, and waste products cross from the capillaries into the mother's blood spaces (*figure 4.21*). The mechanism of transport is variable, as diffusion, facilitated diffusion, osmosis, active transport and pinocytosis all occur (see *Biology 1*, chapter 4). Note that the fetal and maternal blood vessels are not directly connected, so fetal blood does not mix with maternal blood.

SAQ 4.11

Suggest reasons why it would be harmful for there to be direct contact between maternal and fetal blood in the placenta.

SAQ 4.12

Using *figure 4.21* to help you, list the parts of the placenta that are composed of **a** fetal tissue, and **b** maternal tissue.

Overall, the fully developed placenta is a relatively large, pancake-shaped structure. By the end of pregnancy, about 10% of the mother's blood passes through the placenta for each circulation of her body. At birth, it is an average 15–20 cm in diameter and 3 cm thick in the centre. It weighs about 600 g, about one-sixth the weight of the fetus. It becomes detached from the uterus wall at birth and is delivered after the baby as the 'afterbirth'.

Functions of the placenta

The main functions of the placenta are:

> to exchange products between mother and fetus, to make hormones and to act as a protective barrier.

The products listed below are known to move across the placenta (*table 4.2*), but identifying the transfer routes is very difficult. Transport is highly complex, and methods and routes may change during the course of the pregnancy. The role of pinocytosis is particularly difficult to evaluate.

Exchange of materials

■ **Respiratory gases**. Fetal haemoglobin has a higher affinity for oxygen than adult haemoglobin (see *Biology 1*, chapter 8) since the molecule has two alpha and two gamma chains instead of two alpha and two beta chains. This is necessary because the fetus has to 'steal' oxygen from the mother's haemoglobin and also because the concentration (partial pressure) of oxygen in the mother's blood is not as high as in the atmospheric air we breathe. Oxygen diffuses from a higher concentration in the maternal blood space to a lower concentration in the fetal blood, passing through the thin (only one cell thick) walls of the chorionic villi and the capillaries. Waste carbon dioxide diffuses in the opposite direction down its own diffusion gradient.

■ **Nutrients and water**. All essential nutrients pass from maternal to fetal blood, including glucose, amino acids, fatty acids, glycerol, some fats, salts and vitamins. Water can cross by osmosis, due partly to differences in blood pressure, and hence water potential, between mother and fetus. The placenta can also *store* glucose in the form of glycogen as an emergency reserve of carbohydrate for the fetus. The movement of glucose is a good example of facilitated diffusion: it moves down a concentration gradient using a special carrier protein in the plasma membranes. Ions (such as sodium, potassium, calcium and iron), amino acids and vitamins probably cross by active transport. Sodium and potassium can also diffuse across the placenta. Fatty acids may cross by pinocytosis.

- **Excretory products.** Carbon dioxide is an excretory product of fetal respiration. In addition, the fetus excretes nitrogenous waste, such as urea, which diffuses into the mother's blood and is removed by her kidneys.
- **Antibodies.** The placenta allows the transfer of some antibodies from the mother to the fetus. Pinocytosis is probably involved. Thus the fetus gains protection from the same diseases as the mother. This protection lasts for a few months after birth. However, problems can arise with the Rhesus blood group. About 84% of humans have Rhesus antigens in the plasma membranes of their red blood cells (these are also found in Rhesus monkeys, hence the name). Such people are described as **Rhesus positive (Rh+)** whereas the 16% who lack the antigens are described as **Rhesus negative (Rh−)**. If the mother is Rh− and the baby Rh+, there are circumstances, usually with the second or subsequent Rh+ babies, when the mother will make antibodies against the baby's Rhesus antigens. These antibodies can pass from mother to fetus across the placenta, attack the red blood cells of the fetus and make them **agglutinate** (stick together). This will lead to haemolytic disease of the newborn and cause problems such as anaemia and jaundice. Such a situation can be prevented by giving Rh− mothers an injection of anti-Rhesus antibodies shortly after giving birth to their first Rh+ baby. Any Rhesus antigens that have entered her body from the baby are quickly destroyed before she mounts her own immune response. The next time she has a Rh+ baby, her immune system will have no 'memory' of the antigens and not cause agglutination.

Other roles
- **Endocrine organ.** The placenta makes a number of hormones and is therefore part of the **endocrine system**. After three months of pregnancy it takes over from the corpus luteum as the main source of oestrogen and progesterone. *Figure 4.23* summarises the placental hormones and their functions.
- **Protective barrier.** The placenta acts as a barrier to the passage of most pathogens. If the mother suffers a bacterial infection it is therefore not normally passed to the fetus. Some viruses, however, are small enough to cross the placenta. Two common problems are the rubella (German measles) virus and the HIV virus (which can lead to AIDS). Mass vaccination of girls at puberty has almost eradicated rubella in developed countries, but if the fetus *is* infected during the first eight weeks of pregnancy (because the mother catches German measles), the result can be blindness, deafness, heart problems or mental retardation.

Table 4.2 summarises some of the substances that cross the placenta.

SAQ 4.13
Give examples of substances that cross the placenta by the following mechanisms: **a** diffusion; **b** active transport; **c** facilitated diffusion; **d** osmosis; **e** pinocytosis.

The amnion
The **amnion**, like the chorion, is a structure that grows from the developing embryo (*figure 4.21a*). It is tough, thin and transparent and completely surrounds the embryo, and later the developing fetus, throughout its development. The space enclosed, the **amniotic cavity**, becomes filled with a watery liquid, secreted by the amnion and called

	From fetus to mother	From mother to fetus
Of benefit to fetus	CO_2, urea	O_2, nutrients, water, antibodies, antibiotics
Potentially harmful to fetus	antigens, e.g. Rhesus antigen	some viruses, e.g. rubella, HIV; toxins; drugs, e.g. alcohol, crack (cocaine), heroin; tobacco products, e.g. nicotine, carbon monoxide; Rhesus antibodies

- **Table 4.2** Some of the substances that cross the placenta.

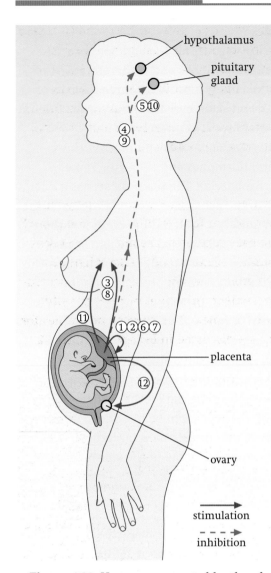

Oestrogen
1 stimulates growth of uterus
2 sensitises uterus to oxytocin
3 stimulates development of duct system of breasts
4 inhibits FSH
5 inhibits release of prolactin, therefore inhibits lactation (secretion of milk) Some prolactin is synthesised before birth, but it is mainly released by the pituitary gland after birth; it stimulates milk secretion
Progesterone
6 maintains lining of uterus (the endometrium)
7 relaxes muscle of uterus (prevents contraction and possible miscarriage)
8 stimulates development of milk glands in breasts ready for lactation
9 inhibits FSH
10 inhibits release of prolactin
Human placental lactogen (HPL)
synthesis gradually increases during pregnancy
11 stimulates growth and development of breasts in preparation for lactation. Needed for oestrogen and progesterone to be effective (3 and 8) Also adjusts glucose and fat metabolism of mother to advantage of fetus
Chorionic gonadotrophin (CG)
12 produced by the chorion from the time the embryo implants. Target is ovary. Maintains corpus luteum up to about 3 months, thus maintaining production of oestrogen and progesterone until placenta takes over this function. Level then declines

● **Figure 4.23** Hormones secreted by the placenta and their functions.

amniotic fluid, in which the fetus is suspended. Its chief function is to protect the embryo or fetus from physical shock and damage. However, it also allows the fetus to move freely, which probably aids the development of muscles and bones. The amniotic fluid is similar in composition to the liquid part of the blood (plasma) of the fetus and mother, except for having a very low protein content and a significantly higher concentration of nitrogenous waste towards the end of pregnancy.

There is constant exchange between the body of the fetus and the amniotic fluid via the respiratory and urinary pathways and the gut. This is important in maintaining the correct volume of amniotic fluid. The fetus swallows amniotic fluid (about 120 cm^3 per hour at week 28). It urinates into the amniotic fluid (reaching a peak of 26 cm^3 per hour by week 40). Until it is about 20 weeks old, exchange can also take place through the skin of the fetus, which has not yet formed its protective dead layer. The fluid may help to maintain a constant temperature around the fetus if the mother is subjected to extremes of temperature for long periods.

The fluid also contains cells that have shed from the surface of the fetus, chorion and amnion, all of which are derived from the original zygote and are therefore genetically identical. This is made use of in the technique of **amniocentesis**, during which amniotic fluid is sampled using a long, hollow needle inserted through the abdominal wall. Chemical analysis of the fluid and examination of fetal cells, for example for chromosomal abnormalities, is a useful guide to certain disorders of the fetus. The technique can, however, carry the risk of triggering a miscarriage.

Actions of the mother that affect fetal development

During the nine months of gestation (pregnancy) the health, activities and environment of the mother affect the fetus in many ways. This is particularly true in the critical period up to the end of the first three months when the major organ systems are being developed. At this stage, the woman may not even know she is pregnant. After the first three months, the fetus mainly has to grow in size and mature. One of the aims of prenatal (antenatal or 'before birth') care is to try to ensure that damage to the fetus is avoided. More recently, emphasis has also been placed on pre*conceptual* advice because relevant life style changes take time to accomplish and should ideally be started before conception. Where possible, positive actions such as sensible levels of exercise, management of stress and a healthy diet are be encouraged, as well as avoiding potentially harmful activities such as smoking. Some factors, such as housing conditions, may be impossible to change. Let us look at some important factors in more detail.

Nutrition

One 'old wives' tale' suggests that the pregnant woman should 'eat for two'. If the size and growth rate of the baby relative to the mother are taken into account, 10% extra food intake might be a very rough guide, but *table 4.3* shows that, according to government guidelines of 1991, the situation is more complex. Dietary reference values for pregnancy are discussed in *Biology 1*, chapter 12.

	Non-pregnant	Pregnant	Notes
energy (MJ)	8.1	8.9*	For growth of fetus, and deposition of fat in mother's body for lactation later (but usually less physical activity late in pregnancy).
protein (g)	36	42	For growth of fetus and maternal tissue, e.g. uterus, breasts.
calcium (mg)	525	525	For bones and teeth and other purposes. (During pregnancy effectiveness of calcium absorption increases, so no extra dietary calcium is normally needed.)
iron (mg)	11.4	11.4	For extra haemoglobin for mother and fetus (pregnant woman has $1.5\,dm^3$ more blood). Anaemia and tiredness result if deficient. (Increased needs are achieved without extra in diet because none lost by menstruation, absorption from gut increases and stores are mobilised. Extra needed if low stores.)
vitamin A (mg)	400	500	For: growth, development and differentiation of fetus; provision of reserves in liver of fetus; maternal tissue growth, particularly healthy skin and epithelia.
thiamin (vitamin B$_1$) (mg)	0.60	0.66	Requirements related to energy needs – helps make energy available.
riboflavin (vitamin B$_2$) (mg)	0.9	1.2	To enable release of energy from food.
nicotinic acid (vitamin B$_3$) (mg)	10.7	11.8	For cell respiration – requirements related to energy needs.
vitamin C (mg)	25	35	For healthy connective tissue. Stimulates absorption of iron.
vitamin D** (mg)	0	0	Stimulates absorption and use of calcium, e.g. for bones and teeth.
folate*** (mg)	150	250	For efficient use of iron and therefore formation of haemoglobin and red blood cells. Pills commonly given as supplement during pregnancy. Any lack leads to a higher incidence of fetal neural tube defects such as spina bifida.

* final 3 months only
** most people who go out in the sun need no dietary source of vitamin D since it is made by the action of light on the skin
*** compounds derived from folic acid

● **Table 4.3** Estimated average requirements per day of nutrients for pregnant and non-pregnant women.

SAQ 4.14

With reference to *table 4.3* **a** What nutrients are needed in greater quantity in the diet during pregnancy? **b** In which cases are more than an extra 10% of normal requirements needed? **c** In which cases where more of a nutrient is needed is the extra *not* supplied by extra consumption? **d** For each of the cases in **a**, **b** and **c**, explain why the extra is required.

Smoking

Tobacco smoke contains a huge number of harmful ingredients, in particular, nicotine, tar (which contains many carcinogens) and carbon monoxide (*Biology 1*, chapter 14). Nicotine and carbon monoxide can cross the placenta easily and are known to affect development of the fetus. (Remember that smoke enters the *mother's* lungs, not the lungs of the fetus, a common error!) If you speak to any midwife or nurse working in intensive baby care units, they will tell you how easy it is to recognise that a mother has been a smoker from the appearance of the placenta and umbilical cord at birth: the umbilical blood vessels are often narrower and the placenta smaller. This helps to explain the fact that smoking mothers are more likely to miscarry and that their babies are often born underweight (on average 200 g underweight if the mother smokes 10–20 cigarettes per day). This phenomenon is common and is known as **intra-uterine growth retardation (IUGR)**. Underweight babies are more at risk if there are subsequent birth complications, so smoking also increases **perinatal mortality** (deaths just before, at, or just after birth). They are also more likely to be born prematurely and are less resistant to infection. Respiratory problems are more common (a sign of immaturity of the lungs). Smoking is also known to significantly reduce vitamin C uptake in the pregnant mother.

As you may remember from *Biology 1*, chapter 8, carbon monoxide binds strongly to haemoglobin (mainly the mother's) to form **carboxyhaemoglobin**. This reduces the oxygen-carrying capacity of the mother, and hence the baby. This in turn slows the growth rate, resulting in an underweight baby. Recent evidence suggests oxygen transport across the placenta is normally accelerated by a carrier molecule and that carbon monoxide may reduce the efficiency of this carrier.

Nicotine causes constriction of blood vessels and the most harmful consequence of this is probably the restriction of blood flow through the placenta, reducing the rate of exchange of nutrients, oxygen and other substances between mother and fetus. Nicotine also stimulates cardiac (heart) muscle and may make the baby's heart beat too fast.

Alcohol

There is a growing trend towards measuring alcohol consumption in terms of grams (g). Measuring it in terms of numbers of drinks per day is not very precise since drink size and alcohol content are variable. To make it easier to calculate intake, 'standard units' are used. One unit equals 8 g of pure alcohol (10 cm^3). One small glass of wine, or a 'short', can be considered as 1 unit, or 8 g of alcohol. This is also roughly equivalent to half a pint of beer, although beers vary from 12–40 g of alcohol per pint.

Alcohol drunk by the mother crosses the placenta easily. It is particularly damaging in the early stages of development, roughly the first eight weeks. Quantities of 80 g or more per day (the equivalent of 10 glasses of wine or five pints of beer or 10 'shorts') may give rise to a condition known as **fetal alcohol syndrome** (FAS). This includes one or more of the following:

- mental retardation;
- reduced growth (before and after birth);
- poor muscle tone (that is the muscles are not in a state of partial contraction ready for action);
- heart defects;
- abnormal limb development;
- certain facial characteristics (such as a short, upturned nose, cleft palate, hare lip or receding chin);
- behavioural problems.

Growth of the infant continues to be slow after birth and problems such as hyperactivity or poor attention span and learning disorders continue in later years.

Although this syndrome is regarded as rare, it is not clear whether there is such a thing as a *safe* level of alcohol for the embryo and fetus. Some experts believe there is not. Other factors are often associated with excessive drinking, such as poor diet and poor living conditions, which make it difficult in practice to study the effects of alcohol in isolation. However, in 1988 a leading embryologist showed that alcohol may even damage eggs *before* conception, raising the chances of miscarriage and the incidence of chromosome abnormalities such as Down's syndrome. Effects can be far more subtle and harder to detect at lower consumption levels. How would you know if you had reduced the IQ of your child by 10 points?

Moderate alcohol consumption seems to be associated with more miscarriages than normal, as well as low birthweight and congenital (at birth) malformations, especially of the nervous system (the brain in particular). For example, women who drink more than 100 g (about 12 units) of alcohol per week have more than twice the risk of delivering an underweight baby compared with those drinking less than 50 g (about 6 units) per week. Low levels of consumption (less than 50 g per week, but no more than 20 g (2.5 units) in a given day) seem to have no detectable consequences.

Other drugs

Most drugs can cross the placenta easily. Common pharmaceutical drugs such as aspirin, codeine, paracetamol and sleeping pills (barbiturates) cause no known damage to the fetus if recommended doses are taken. However, since drugs are likely to affect the fetus as well as the mother, doctors may advise avoiding all drugs if possible.

The, sadly, classic and most dramatic example of a prescribed drug that has caused problems is thalidomide. This was introduced in the early 1960s as a remedy for morning sickness (nausea), which can be particularly serious in some women. Within two years about 7000 children were born with severe physical disabilities as a result, limb development being particularly affected. The procedures for the testing of new drugs have since been changed to try to ensure that no similar tragedy occurs again. In any case, women should always consult a doctor before taking any medicine during pregnancy.

Whether prescribed or not, drugs can have serious effects on the fetus if misused. If the mother is dependent on a drug such as heroin or crack (cocaine), then her baby probably will be as well. Such babies are five times more likely to be born underweight and are twice as likely to be premature, with the associated dangers already discussed. Birth problems and miscarriages are also more common. A drug-addicted baby is a pathetic sight and needs intensive care in a hospital. Although most survive, painful withdrawal symptoms occur over the first two weeks of life in 60–90% of babies born to drug-dependent mothers. These can affect the baby's normal reflexes, such as the sucking reflex, the body may be rigid, uncontrolled tremors may be experienced and 'cot deaths' are more common.

Disease

As some disease-causing organisms can cross the placenta (page 71), particular care should be taken to avoid these. Of particular importance are the rubella, HIV and hepatitis B viruses. In the UK both hepatitis B and the HIV virus are often associated with injecting drug abusers, spreading when contaminated needles and syringes are used. Both can also be spread sexually and, along with a range of other sexually transmitted diseases, can also be passed on to the baby as it passes through the vagina at birth. Vaccination against hepatitis B is expensive, and as yet there is no vaccination against the HIV virus.

Preconceptual and antenatal care

Parents-to-be, both mothers and fathers, can take a positive step by attending antenatal classes. The health of both the unborn child and the mother can then be monitored and relevant advice given. Increased antenatal care has led to a significant drop in perinatal mortality (that is, death at around the time of birth). More recently, preconceptual care for couples has been encouraged by the government and the medical profession, so that relevant advice on topics such as giving up smoking, health checks, folic acid supplements and genetic counselling can be given before pregnancy even begins. It is hoped that the incidence of malformations of babies in England and Wales will thus be reduced from the current level of 2.5 per 100 live births.

Abortion

Abortion is the premature termination of pregnancy, resulting in death of the embryo or fetus. It may happen naturally, in which case it is generally called a **miscarriage**, **spontaneous abortion** or **natural abortion**. On the other hand, when carried out deliberately, it may be called **induced abortion**. In this book the term abortion is used to mean induced abortion.

Until 1968, abortion was illegal in the UK. The Abortion Act, which made abortion legal under certain circumstances, came into force in April 1968 and was modified in April 1991. Since 1968, more than three million abortions are known to have been carried out in the UK. Overall about 20% of conceptions in the UK are now terminated by abortion.

Under the Act, the maximum age at which a fetus can be aborted is 24 weeks, with the exception that, in cases of severe fetal abnormality or serious risk to the health or life of the mother, abortion may be carried out at any stage of pregnancy. The full legal grounds for abortion are one or more of:

■ risk to the woman's life (abortion at any time);
■ risk of grave permanent injury to the physical or mental health of the woman (abortion at any time);
■ risk of injury to the physical or mental health of the woman (up to 24 weeks) (the most commonly used grounds for abortion);
■ risk of injury to the physical or mental health of existing children (up to 24 weeks);
■ substantial risk of a child being born seriously disabled (abortion at any time);
■ emergencies (abortion at any time).

Also, two medical practitioners must agree to the abortion – it cannot be just one person's decision.

The most important reason given for legalising abortion in the UK was that it would reduce the number of unsafe abortions. Before 1968, many women died or were permanently injured as a result of having illegal abortions in non-sterile conditions or being damaged by inexpert surgery. Legalisation, it was argued, would reduce the health risks to, and financial exploitation of, women and would also avoid the danger of the

Age of woman	Number of women having abortions in 1996
under 16	3645
16–19	28790
20–24	46356
25–29	39311
30–34	28228
35–39	16118
40–44	5027
45+	428
not stated	13

● **Table 4.4** Age of women at time of abortion in 1996 (residents of England and Wales).

law being 'brought into disrepute' by being constantly ignored. These and other ethical issues are examined later.

SAQ 4.15

a From *table 4.4*, in what maternal age group do most abortions occur?

b Plot bar charts of the data in *table 4.4*.

c Calculate the number of women in each age category as a percentage of the total.

Methods of abortion

Five methods of abortion are in general use, the method used in a particular case depending mainly on the stage of pregnancy. The first, second and fourth methods listed below all involve a local or general anaesthetic.

■ **Vacuum aspiration** – up to 12 weeks of pregnancy. This is the most common method and is relatively safe and easy, taking about 30 minutes. The cervix is stretched, a narrow, flexible tube is inserted into the uterus and the fetal material is gently sucked out with a pump (aspirator). A variation of the technique, **menstrual aspiration**, takes only about five minutes and can be done up to six weeks after conception. A smaller tube can be used, so dilation of the cervix is not necessary. In this case the uterus lining is gently sucked out with a small syringe.

■ **Dilation and curettage (D + C)** – at 12–16 weeks of pregnancy. The cervix is dilated and the lining of the uterus scraped with a spoon-

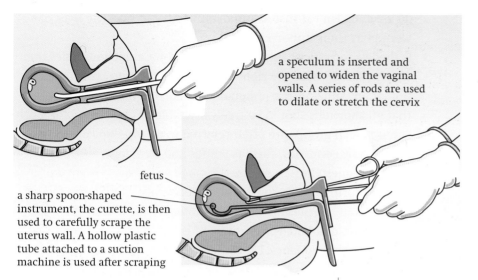

a speculum is inserted and opened to widen the vaginal walls. A series of rods are used to dilate or stretch the cervix

fetus

a sharp spoon-shaped instrument, the curette, is then used to carefully scrape the uterus wall. A hollow plastic tube attached to a suction machine is used after scraping

● **Figure 4.24** Dilation and curettage.

shaped curette (knife) to remove the fetus. The contents can be finally sucked out using vacuum aspiration (*figure 4.24*).

■ **Prostaglandins** or **saline injection** – at 16+ weeks of pregnancy. Prostaglandins or saline solution are injected through the abdominal wall into the amniotic fluid. Prostaglandins are naturally occurring hormones which in high concentration cause uterine contractions. This kills the fetus. The woman must then go through an induced labour to deliver the dead fetus because it is too large to be removed by aspiration. This method is probably more distressing than the methods above.

■ **Hysterotomy (Caesarean section)** – at 16+ weeks of pregnancy. This is performed only on rare occasions because the physical risk to the mother is greater than with other methods. It is only used if other methods cannot be used or are unsuccessful. The fetus is removed through a cut in the abdominal wall and uterus, as with a Caesarean birth.

■ **RU486 (the 'morning-after' pill)** – at less than 10 weeks of pregnancy. RU486 is an anti-progesterone drug which results in the rejection of the embryo or fetus. Its long-term effects are unknown. Three tablets are taken to start the procedure. Then one or two days later, a prostaglandin injection or pessary is given which causes uterine contractions and completes termination. It is cheaper and less invasive than alternative abortion methods.

Using modern techniques, the physical health risk to the woman of having an abortion is less, on average, than that of completing the pregnancy. Day-care abortion is performed on an outpatient basis and usually enables a woman to return home three to four hours after the operation. The earlier an abortion is carried out, the less likely are medical complications.

If the uterus or oviducts become infected, pelvic inflammatory disease, with possible infertility, is the most common complication. Other possible complications include the increased likelihood of future **ectopic** pregnancy (the development of the fetus in the oviduct or peritoneal cavity rather than in the uterus), a stretched and non-functional cervix, the perforation of the uterus, and retention of the placenta, leading to bleeding. An average of five women die each year from legal abortions in England and Wales and about 5% are made sterile by the operation. This compares with thousands of deaths and injuries pre-legalisation.

Ethical issues of abortion

As we have seen, the law is an attempt to balance some difficult ethical considerations. Being literally a matter of life and death, it is not surprising that strong views are commonly held. Some of the numerous issues involved are discussed below, but full debate here is not possible.

1 Is abortion murder? Many people of the Islamic and Christian faiths would say that it is, because they believe that the soul is independent of the body and is present from the moment of conception. For others it is a much more difficult question to answer. A common argument is that the fetus must reach a certain level of complexity before abortion should be regarded as murder.

Some 'Pro-Life' groups want the time limit on abortion lowered to 18 weeks, arguing, for example, that after 18 weeks a fetus feels pain, but no-one knows for certain when the subjective experience of pain develops. Many Pro-Life groups are totally against abortion (*figure 4.25a*). Should such groups make any exceptions, for example for a woman who has become pregnant after being raped?

2   An estimated two million women die worldwide each year from illegal or unsafe abortions. Legalising abortion results in fewer deaths and harmful side-effects on health (*figure 4.26*). Isn't it just as important to try to save the lives of women as their unborn babies?

3   Is the law too strict? The National Abortion Campaign argues that women should have the right to choose whether to have an abortion at any time during pregnancy – 'abortion on demand' – and that all abortions should be freely available on the National Health Service. Such groups are often referred to as 'Pro-Choice' (*figure 4.25b*). Many countries, such as France and Denmark, allow abortion on request. In some countries, such as Russia, it is virtually the only form of birth control and the average woman has several abortions in her lifetime. Many arguments can be used to support abortion on demand. For example, it is a woman's own body that is affected by pregnancy. Unwanted children tend to do less well in education, employment and partnerships. An extra child may cause family problems especially in cases of poverty.

4   Is the 24-week deadline appropriate? Twenty-four weeks represents the age at which the fetus can be expected to survive outside the mother's womb with medical assistance. It is the limit which receives most support from the public. To a biologist, though, it is a fairly arbitrary dividing line because the main problem preventing independent survival of the fetus just before 24 weeks is only the immaturity of its lungs. Should permission to carry out abortion be at all related to the ability of the fetus to survive independently outside the womb? The latter depends on the present limits of our technology. Should the right of the fetus to life depend on our technological development?

5   Is the law strict enough? It is relatively easy to get an abortion on grounds of risk to the mother and more than 170 000 are carried out each year in the UK.

6   Should more be done to try to reduce the number of abortions by promoting birth control? Many women are pressured into abortion because they are not in a relationship, (in 1990, 8% of abortions were from conceptions within marriage and 36% from

● **Figure 4.25**
a An anti-abortion rally.
b A pro-choice rally.

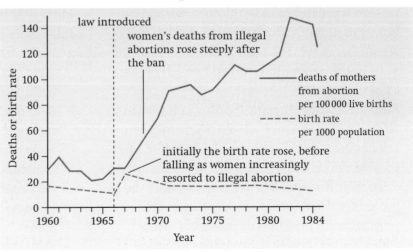

● **Figure 4.26** Effects of an anti-abortion law introduced in 1966 in Romania.

conceptions outside marriage). Should official attitudes to single mothers change? Should society make it easier for single parents to find work, guaranteeing crêche and nursery places?

7 Does using abortion to terminate disabled fetuses lead to an uncaring attitude within society and the alienation of disabled people? Or does it, as some believe, demonstrate a *caring* attitude?

8 Should the father have any rights in deciding whether an abortion should go ahead? At present, he has none.

9 Abortion poses some health risks to the mother, both physical and psychological, although on average these are less than if the pregnancy goes ahead. Many women suffer feelings of guilt and regret afterwards and may need counselling. These feelings can return after several years.

10 Should a mother be encouraged to give up a baby for adoption at birth rather than have an abortion?

In vitro fertilisation

Having looked at normal reproduction and prevention and termination of pregnancy, we now consider one way of treating the inability to reproduce. **In vitro fertilisation (IVF)** is commonly known as the **test tube baby** technique. The first successful use of the technique came with the birth of Louise Brown in 1978. The term *in vitro* means, literally, 'in glass' and refers to the fact that fertilisation (fusion of the sperm with the egg) takes place *outside* the body. It usually takes place in a glass or plastic dish, and not the proverbial test tube. The technique can be used as a treatment for the following causes of infertility.

- Blocked or damaged oviducts. This can be a result of scar tissue forming in response to infection or abdominal surgery, or it may be an in-born error.
- Failure to produce eggs. Donor eggs can be fertilised and implanted.
- The male has very low sperm counts or poor sperm motility, which will make normal intercourse unlikely to succeed. Fewer sperm are needed to fertilise eggs *in vitro*.

- The woman's cervical mucus is 'hostile', either killing or preventing the passage of sperm.
- The woman has been previously sterilised.

The technique may also be used if it is desirable to screen embryos for genetic defects before allowing pregnancy to proceed. An outline of the procedure is given as follows. Also see *figure 4.27*.

Procedure

Preliminary tests and counselling are carried out to ensure suitability for treatment. Then from the beginning of the menstrual cycle, the woman being treated is injected daily with a hormone, such as FSH, that stimulates the growth of *many* eggs instead of the usual one. This increases the chances of success later. Progress in development of the egg follicles is followed by use of ultra-sound scanning.

Just before ovulation, the 'ripe' eggs are collected, most commonly by **laparoscopy**, performed under general anaesthetic. A narrow telescope is inserted through a tiny cut at the base of the navel into the abdominal cavity, which is inflated with carbon dioxide gas to make viewing easier. A fibre-optic cable connected to a micro-scope and TV monitor outside the body enables the surgeon to observe the internal organs. A long, fine, hollow needle is then inserted into the abdomen just above the pubic hairline, and the eggs are sucked from the follicles. The male partner produces a sperm sample and the most motile sperm are collected from the sample.

The eggs are then 'matured' in an incubator for 4–24 hours in a special sterile culture medium. When they are mature, the sperm are added to the eggs and left for 24 hours for fertilisation to take place. The process of fertilisation can be assisted in a number of ways if sperm activity is low. The zona pellucida can be deliberately damaged to allow easier access of the sperm to the egg, or the sperm are micro-injected through the zona pellucida (a technique known as subzonal insemination, or SUZI) or directly into the cytoplasm of the egg. Two to three days later, any embryos that have formed are examined and a guideline maximum of three suitable embryos are transferred into the uterus of the woman using a soft tube inserted through the vagina and cervix.

● **Figure 4.27** A human egg cell in a pippette prior to IVF.

The fate of any remaining embryos will already have been decided by the couple during preliminary counselling (see later).

SAQ 4.16

Why are freshly ejaculated sperm incapable of fertilising an egg?

Ethical issues of IVF

In vitro fertilisation raises a number of important ethical issues. Probably the most important is the fate of unused embryos. These can be frozen and stored for future use, disposed of, or used for research, depending on the wishes of the couple. There is some evidence that freezing mouse embryos may cause long-term behavioural changes in animals that develop from them. Disposal of human embryos could be regarded as murder. In the UK, research on embryos is allowed only up to 14 days. Up to this time twins can develop, and also the first rudiments of the nervous system appear at 14 days. The research is valuable not just for improving infertility treatment for both men and women, but for developing techniques such as the diagnosis of genetic disease, gene manipulation and stem cell research. It can also be used to investigate reasons for miscarriage. It is worth noting that something like half of all natural pregnancies do not proceed as a result of failure of the embryo to implant.

The success rate of IVF in the UK is only about 15–20%, but is rising. Even though couples are counselled beforehand, failure can be devastating, particularly after the lengthy treatment and many visits to the clinic. Few National Health Service clinics offer the treatment and private treatment is expensive. Apart from the obvious financial burden, particularly since more than one attempt may be necessary, there is the possibility that couples could be exploited in situations where the technique is even less likely to succeed than usual.

There is a risk of multiple pregnancy if more than one of the embryos introduced into the uterus develops. There is no evidence that children born as a result of IVF have a higher than average incidence of abnormalities.

The technique allows the possibility of embryo donation whereby the embryo is donated to another woman. This is basically an early form of adoption, whereby the adopting mother can give birth to the baby. Similarly, either eggs or sperm can be donated to other people. Such gamete donation raises ethical issues which are outside the scope of this book.

SUMMARY

◆ The human reproductive system is closely linked with the excretory system in both sexes. The two systems are known collectively as the urinogenital system.

◆ Secondary oocytes, which later become female gametes (eggs) are produced in the ovaries; male gametes, sperm, are produced in the testes. Ovaries and testes are known as gonads.

◆ Formation of gametes is known as gametogenesis. It involves meiosis of the nuclei of diploid mother cells. Sperm are formed continuously in the walls of the seminiferous tubules. Eggs are produced in cycles, at the rate of approximately one egg per month. The cycle is known as the menstrual cycle.

◆ Gametogenesis is controlled by hormones. The control centre is the hypothalamus, closely linked with the anterior lobe of the pituitary gland. The hypothalamus secretes GnRH (gonadotrophin releasing hormone) which stimulates release of gonadotrophins from the pituitary. These in turn stimulate the gonads.

◆ The gonadotrophic hormones are FSH and LH (also called ICSH in the male). In response to these the gonads produce hormones and gametes. The male hormones are testosterone and inhibin; the female hormones are oestrogen and progesterone. These regulate gonadotrophin production, and thus gametogenesis, by negative feedback.

◆ Fertilisation, the fusion of a sperm with an egg, occurs in the oviduct. Sperm are adapted to swim to the oviduct in the female after sexual intercourse, and to penetrate the follicle cells and zona pellucida around the egg. This penetration involves the acrosome reaction; capacitation of the sperm must take place before it is possible.

◆ Human intervention into the normal reproductive process is common and increasing. Examples are contraception, abortion and *in vitro* fertilisation. All these processes involve ethical dilemmas.

◆ Development of the fetus inside the mother is made possible by an organ unique to mammals, the placenta. It contains tissues from both mother and fetus and allows beneficial exchange of nutrients, respiratory gases, nitrogenous waste and some other substances between the two.

◆ Various transport mechanisms are involved in the placenta, including osmosis, diffusion, facilitated diffusion, active transport and pinocytosis.

◆ Some harmful substances, such as certain drugs and viruses, can cross the placenta. It is therefore important that the mother is aware of how her actions and environment can benefit or damage the fetus.

◆ The placenta also acts as an endocrine organ, secreting chorionic gonadotrophin, oestrogen, progesterone and human placental lactogen. These help to maintain the uterus in a suitable state and stimulate breast development as well as having other important functions.

◆ The fetus is suspended in amniotic fluid inside the amniotic cavity. It is thereby protected from physical shock and damage.

Questions

1 Explain how the structure of the placenta is adapted to its functions.

2 What advice would you give a pregnant woman concerning her diet?

3 Describe the changes that the following cells and their descendants must undergo before fertilisation is possible:
   a primary spermatocyte,
   b primary oocyte.

4 Some states in the USA have considered introducing laws to forcibly confine drug-dependent pregnant women during pregnancy to try to protect the unborn baby. What advantages and disadvantages can you think of for such legislation?

5 a What arguments could you use to try to persuade a woman to give up smoking during pregnancy?
   b Suggest ways in which the Government could encourage pregnant women not to smoke.

6 Discuss the advantages and disadvantages of increasing the availability of contraception worldwide.

7 a Contraceptives can prevent ovulation, fertilisation after ovulation, or implantation. Give examples of each type and explain the biological reason why contraception is achieved in each case.
   b Discuss the health implications of different forms of contraception.

8 a Describe ways in which hormones can be used by the medical profession to regulate and control human fertility.
   b Discuss the potential benefits and problems associated with the use of hormones in this way.

9 If you could change the law on abortion in the UK, what changes would you make, and why?

10 Explain how there can be economic, social and political aspects to the ethical issues associated with IVF.

11 Using the data provided in *table 4.5*, calculate the percentage of abortions carried out on single and married women in the years 1982, 1985, 1990, and 1992. Comment on the trend.

Year	Single	Married	Other (widowed, divorced, separated, unknown)
1982	71 836	40 510	16 207
1985	87 213	37 698	16 190
1990	116 150	38 151	19 599
1992	105 630	36 394	18 471
1997	114 900	33 600	19 300

● **Table 4.5** Marital status of women having abortions in 1982, 1985, 1990, 1992 and 1997 (residents of England and Wales).

Control of growth and reproduction

By the end of this chapter you should be able to:

1 explain the factors that control flowering in short-day and long-day plants;

2 describe the use of plant growth regulators in fruit maturation;

3 design and carry out investigations to identify the major factors affecting germination;

4 describe the reasons for, and the advantages of, seed dormancy;

5 explain the role of plant growth regulators in the control of seed dormancy;

6 describe the role of hormones in birth and lactation;

7 outline the role of hormones in premenstrual tension, the menopause and hormone replacement therapy;

8 outline the roles of the hypothalamus and pituitary gland in human growth and development;

9 describe the structure of the thyroid gland and the functions of thyroxine, the hormone it secretes;

10 describe the control of thyroxine secretion.

In chapter 1 we studied growth and in chapters 2, 3 and 4, reproduction. In this chapter we shall examine some of the chemical control systems that regulate growth and reproduction in both flowering plants and humans.

Genes, environment and coordination

Two major influences are at work in controlling the growth and reproduction of living organisms: their genes and their environment. Important environmental factors include light, temperature, and the availability of nutrients and water. Ultimately, though, it is genes, in the form of DNA, that have the blueprint for successful growth and reproduction. Complex internal coordination and control is required, both to express the DNA blueprint and to respond appropriately to the environment. Plants

rely entirely on chemicals, whereas animals use chemicals, called hormones, *and* a nervous system. In this chapter we shall concentrate on the chemical control systems. In the first part of the chapter we shall focus on plants and use as examples flowering, fruit maturation, germination and dormancy. These processes provide excellent examples of how chemical control of growth and reproduction in plants is closely linked to, and influenced by, environmental change. In the second part of this chapter, hormonal control in animals is illustrated by examples of the control of human reproduction and growth.

Control in plants

Plants rely entirely on chemicals for the internal coordination of growth and development. The chemicals concerned are referred to as **plant growth regulators** or **plant growth substances** or, sometimes, as hormones. There are five classes of plant growth regulator. Three act as growth promoters (auxins, gibberellins and cytokinins) and two as growth inhibitors (abscisic acid and ethene), and they interact to produce their effects.

Flowering

How does a plant 'know' when to flower? You may well have assumed that it simply flowers when it has reached a certain stage of maturity, but this is not necessarily the case. It is often dependent on environmental conditions. Flowering is a very fundamental switch in activity. The flower parts first have to be produced at shoot meristems where leaves and lateral buds are normally produced, so some fundamental change in gene expression must be brought about. The genes that trigger production of flowers must be switched on and other genes switched off. Flowering is therefore of great interest to plant physiologists, and more recently to molecular biologists and geneticists as well. It has important commercial implications because plant growers would welcome the opportunity to be able to switch flowering on or off at will so that they can produce flowers and fruits out of season.

Photoperiodism

In 1910 it was discovered that the length of day (or to be more accurate, the length of time during which there is daylight) seemed to be involved in the flowering response. Moving away from the equator into temperate latitudes, the length of day shows increasing variation during the year. It is an almost constant 12 hours every day of the year at the equator, but varies between 9 and 15 hours in the UK. Length of day is known as the **photoperiod** and the ability to respond to it is called **photoperiodism**. In 1920, N.W. Garner and H.A. Allard showed that tobacco plants would flower only after exposure to a series of short days. This occurs naturally in autumn in the UK, but can be induced in a greenhouse using artificial seven-hour days. Plants like tobacco were called **short-day plants (SDPs)**. Investigations of other

plants revealed that some, such as spinach, would flower only in response to long days (**long-day plants** or **LDPs**). Some were unaffected by day length (**day-neutral plants**).

The other obvious environmental variable, temperature, was also investigated and was found to have a modifying effect on flowering in some cases. For example, some plants were day-neutral at one temperature but not at another.

The next important advance in understanding came in 1938 when K.C. Hamner and J. Bonner discovered that it was *not* day length that the plants were sensitive to! It was the length of the dark period. Thus SDPs ought strictly to be called long-night plants and LDPs should be called short-night plants, although the terms SDP and LDP are still used.

SAQ 5.1
Why might a link between flowering and day length be an advantage to a plant?

SAQ 5.2
What other environmental variable would be a useful cue for plants to flower?

SAQ 5.3
How could you prove that night length rather than day length is the critical factor?

If an SDP such as cocklebur (*Xanthium*) is given long nights, it flowers. However, Hamner and Bonner discovered that if the long night is interrupted by a short light period, flowering is prevented. Even an interruption of a few seconds can be long enough if the light is of a sufficiently high intensity. Similarly, an LDP, such as *Iris*, can be induced to flower in short days if the long night is interrupted by light.

Phytochrome and the action spectrum

Investigators then set about trying to discover which wavelength of light was responsible for reversing the effect of a long night, because this could help identify the pigment responsible for absorbing the light. *Figure 5.1* shows an action

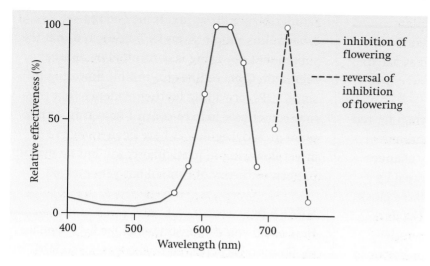

● **Figure 5.1** Action spectra for the effects of a light interruption of the long dark period on flowering in cocklebur (*Xanthium*).

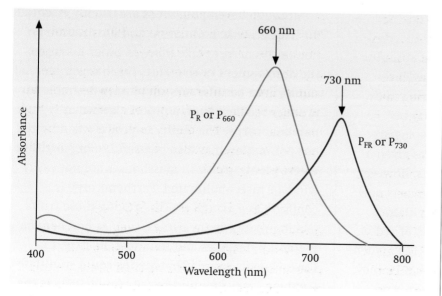

● **Figure 5.2** Experiments in controlling flowering.

● **Figure 5.3** Absorption spectra of the two forms of phytochrome.

spectrum for preventing flowering in cocklebur. It was found that red light was most effective (with a wavelength of 620–660 nm); only two minutes' exposure was required to completely inhibit flowering. Later it was unexpectedly found that far-red light (730 nm) was effective in cancelling out the effect of red light. In a series of light exposures, for example red, far-red, red, far-red, it was always the *final* stimulus that was effective. Flowering could be switched on and off (*figure 5.2*).

This effect was later shown to be due to a pigment, named **phytochrome**. This was isolated in 1964 and shown to exist in two forms, a red-absorbing form, P_R or P_{660} (its absorption peak is 660 nm) and a far-red absorbing form, P_{FR} or P_{730} (absorption peak 730 nm). The absorption spectra of the two forms are shown in *figure 5.3*. Note how closely they match the action spectrum in *figure 5.1*. Phytochrome is a blue-green pigment and, as with haemoglobin, the pigment is mainly a protein. It is present in minute amounts throughout the plant, particularly in the growing tips, and it is involved in a range of plant responses to light, including the greening of leaves. (Note that it is *not* a plant growth regulator.)

Absorption of light by one form of phytochrome converts it rapidly and reversibly to the other form:

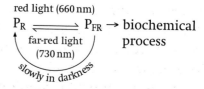

SAQ 5.4
Summarise the difference between an action spectrum and an absorption spectrum. (You may like to look back at *Biology 2*, chapter 1.)

Sunlight contains a lot more red light than far-red light. Therefore during the day, phytochrome exists in the P_{FR} form. At night it slowly changes back to the P_R form. This can be accelerated by using far-red light. In effect, the plant has a clock by which it can measure the length of the dark period: the longer the dark period, the more P_R. The reverse conversion of P_R to P_{FR} in the day or in red light is, in contrast, more like a switch, because it happens rapidly. The P_{FR} form is thought to be the physiologically active form and the P_R form is the inactive form. Assuming this is the case, let us examine how flowering is controlled in LDPs and SDPs.

An LDP will by definition flower if given short nights. We know that at the end of a short night, there will still be some P_{FR} present, as it is converted only slowly to P_R in darkness. LDPs, therefore, probably flower in response to the presence of P_{FR}. An SDP will flower if given *long* nights, by which time all of the P_{FR} will have been converted to P_R. This suggests that the P_{FR} normally *inhibits* flowering, which only occurs in the absence of such inhibition.

Unfortunately for the validity of this theory, exposure to far-red light does not completely substitute for long nights, so some other, as yet unknown, factor also appears to be important.

Growth regulators in flowering

It was shown in the 1930s that the light stimulus controlling flowering is perceived by the leaves and somehow transmitted to the flowering apex. This implies that a growth regulator may be involved. So convinced were plant physiologists that this regulator must exist that it was given a name, **florigen**. Despite intensive efforts, however, it has never been isolated and its existence is now in doubt. However, a class of growth regulators called **gibberellins** can mimic the effect of red light in promoting flowering in certain LDPs, such as henbane, which are rosette plants (that is, they grow close to the ground). These plants must 'bolt', in other words the stem must elongate

rapidly, before flowering. It may be that gibberellins simply promote bolting and that the subsequent flowering is controlled by another regulator. Gibberellins also inhibit flowering in some SDPs, providing further evidence that they may sometimes help to control flowering. Other plant growth regulators have been known to affect flowering in particular cases, but no overall pattern or theory of control has yet emerged.

SAQ 5.5
How could you demonstrate that the light stimulus for flowering is perceived by the leaves in a SDP?

Fruit maturation

Agriculture is the world's largest industry and fruits of various kinds are among the most important products. There is therefore a great deal of commercial interest in the process of fruit development and ripening. Usually, pollination, or pollination followed by fertilisation to produce seeds, is necessary to trigger the development of the fruit. Germinating pollen is a rich source of a class of plant growth regulators known as **auxins** (see *Biology 2*, chapter 6). Pollination also seems to activate auxin production by the parts of the gynoecium such as the style and the ovules. Seeds are rich sources of two other groups of growth regulators, the **gibberellins** and **cytokinins**, both of which may be involved in fruit maturation.

Although developing seeds are usually essential for fruit growth, pollination and fertilisation do not always need to take place in order to trigger the development of the fruit. This has commercial significance because it is sometimes desirable to produce seedless fruit, a process known as **parthenocarpy**. The ability to produce fruit without pollination may also be useful in horticulture where plants grown in glasshouses are not easily wind- or insect-pollinated. Parthenocarpy is common as a *natural* process among those fruits which produce many ovules, such as figs, bananas, melons, pineapples and tomatoes. In 1939, F.G. Gustafson discovered that auxins could stimulate parthenocarpy in a number of plants, such as the tomato. Pollen grain extracts can sometimes do the same. This links well with the involvement of auxins in pollination noted above. It has also been shown that the horticulturally chosen varieties of bananas, pineapples, oranges and grapes which are *naturally* parthenocarpic have unusually high levels of auxins compared with non-parthenocarpic fruits where, presumably, the seeds contribute the extra auxins needed for fruit development. Evidence for the suggestion that seeds contribute auxins is provided by the experiment illustrated in *figure 5.4*.

Gibberellins will induce parthenocarpy in a few fruits which are unaffected by auxins. They are more effective than auxins at promoting parthenocarpy in tomatoes. A gibberellin is being used commercially to increase the size of seedless grapes, since naturally seedless grapes tend to be small and suitable mainly for raisin production rather than for eating.

Synthetic auxins, made commercially in a laboratory, are used to improve fruit set and fruit size, for example in grapes. **Fruit set** is the triggering

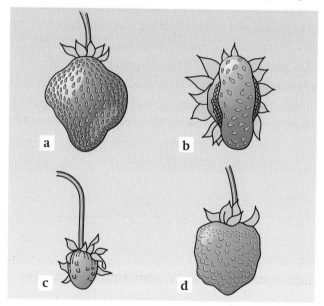

● **Figure 5.4** The control of flesh growth in the strawberry.
a A normal strawberry with the 'seeds' left on.
b When some of the 'seeds' are removed growth of the flesh occurs only under the 'seeds' which remain.
c Growth is stopped when all 'seeds' are removed.
d Growth is restored when the seedless strawberry is treated with auxins. Significant quantities of auxins can be extracted from the strawberry 'seeds'.
Note that the fleshy part of the strawberry is really the receptacle. Each pip is a fruit with a seed inside it.

of the development of the embryo, which in turn leads to successful development of the fruit. In natural situations there is sometimes a heavy shedding from the plant of young fruit that has not set, with a consequent loss in yield. The commercial advantages of preventing this are great. Gibberellins are also used to increase fruit set, particularly in mandarins, tangerines and pears.

Fruit ripening

One of the difficulties in marketing fruit is trying to ensure that ripening takes place at just the right time to appeal to the customer. When you buy bananas, for example, you may well want the option of buying them slightly under-ripe or you may want them ready to eat. Days or weeks spent in transit therefore pose problems. What is needed is an understanding of the ripening process so that it can be artificially regulated.

As long ago as the 1930s it was known that the gas **ethene** speeds up the ripening of citrus fruits such as lemons. Later it was shown that ripe bananas and apples, and a whole range of other fruits, release ethene gas naturally. We now know that ethene is a natural growth regulator that can probably be made by all plant organs. It is a simple organic molecule, with the formula C_2H_4. It is regarded as a **growth inhibitor** and stimulates the plant's ageing processes. It is particularly associated with leaf fall, fruit ripening and fruit fall.

Fruit ripening can be regarded as a senescence (ageing) process. It is typically accompanied by a burst of respiratory activity, which seems to be controlled by the ethene. This process requires oxygen and can therefore be inhibited by lack of oxygen. Thus we have the principle by which fruit ripening can be artificially controlled. Fruits can be picked before they are ripe and prevented from ripening by storage in an atmosphere lacking oxygen, usually on the ships during the sea voyage. Then, when ripening is required just before sending the fruit to market, it can be stimulated by adding oxygen and ethene. This method is applied commercially to bananas and citrus fruits. Ethene is also used to stimulate ripening of tomatoes.

Table 5.1 summarises some of the commercial uses of auxins, gibberellins and ethene.

Growth regulator	Commercial use
Auxins (including synthetic auxins)	Induce seedless fruit (parthenocarpy). Avoid need for pollination. Improve fruit set, e.g. apples, holly. Increase fruit size, e.g. grapes.
Gibberellins	Induce seedless fruit (parthenocarpy) in a few plants, e.g. grapes. Avoid need for pollination. Improve fruit set, e.g. mandarins, tangerines, pears. Increase fruit size, e.g. grapes. Break dormancy of cereal seeds, e.g. barley in brewing.
Ethene	Controls ripening, e.g. bananas, citrus fruits, tomatoes.

● **Table 5.1** Some commercial uses of auxins, gibberellins and ethene in fruit maturation and seed dormancy.

Seed dormancy

Dormancy is the state where germination will not occur, even if environmental conditions are favourable.

It is often an advantage for a seed to undergo a period of dormancy. Germination can then be linked to important factors such as a favourable season. For example, a seed released in autumn is more likely to germinate successfully if it remains dormant throughout winter, even if conditions for growth are favourable in autumn. Seeds of desert plants commonly remain dormant until a rainy spell. A dormancy period also allows more time for dispersal. Some of the common mechanisms for controlling dormancy are discussed below.

Growth inhibitors

Some seeds, such as ash, contain growth inhibitors, usually either in the seed coat (testa) or in the embryo. **Abscisic acid (ABA)** (*Biology 2*, chapter 6) is the most common inhibitor. However, a wide variety of chemicals act as inhibitors, from sodium chloride (high concentrations of which

cause osmotic inhibition in some seeds) to complex organic compounds such as essential oils and alkaloids. The inhibitors may be lost gradually by being leached out by water, or their effects may be overcome by growth promoters such as gibberellins. Alternatively, if the testa is preventing the escape of the inhibitors, the testa may have to be damaged. Many fruits contain inhibitors that prevent the seeds germinating while still inside the fruit. One such example is the tomato and, indeed, tomato juice is a potent growth inhibitor of the seeds of many species.

SAQ 5.6
Why would the need for leaching of inhibitors from its seeds be an appropriate control mechanism for the germination of a desert plant?

Prechilling

Many seeds require an exposure to low temperatures in moist conditions with oxygen for several weeks or months before they will germinate, a process known as **prechilling**. Cereals, peach, plum, cherry and apple are examples (*figure 5.5*). This prevents the seeds from germinating in autumn or during a warm spell in winter. The mechanism is still unclear and probably varies from species to species. The latest evidence

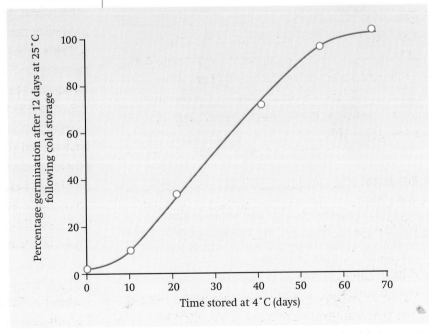

● **Figure 5.5** Germination of apple seeds after different periods of storage at 4°C.

suggests that it is the embryo that is sensitive to the low-temperature stimulus. Adding gibberellins sometimes substitutes for prechilling, so perhaps prechilling brings about a natural increase in gibberellins in some species.

Light

Light is an important factor in controlling the germination of the seeds of many wild plants. Light *stimulates* the germination of many seeds, for instance lilac and some varieties of lettuce (see *box 5B* on page 90). On the other hand, the germination of the seeds of some other species is *inhibited* by light.

SAQ 5.7

Humans have tended to select out the sensitivity to light from the seeds of crop plants. Suggest a reason for this.

SAQ 5.8

Suggest a reason for the fact that light-stimulated seeds are often small and without large food reserves.

SAQ 5.9

Suggest an advantage for a seed whose germination is inhibited by light.

SAQ 5.10

When light passes through leaves, most of the red and blue wavelengths are absorbed, but most of the far-red light passes through. Far-red light often inhibits germination of seeds that require normal sunlight for germination. Suggest an ecological advantage for this.

SAQ 5.11

Which pigment is responsible for the far-red light inhibiting effect?

Scarification

Some seeds require physical damage to the testa before germination. Such damage is called **scarification**. Without it, the testa may be so tough that it prevents growth or may prevent

● **Figure 5.6** A forest fire in Western Australia.

oxygen or water uptake. This can be overcome by artificially scarifying the seeds; sandpaper and knives have been used, but sometimes even a pin prick is sufficient.

The phenomenon is ecologically important. For example, certain species can be stimulated to germinate by exposure to fire. The seeds of one species of *Albizzia*, an Australian tree of the legume (pea and bean) family, contain a small plug in the seed coat which pops out when the seed is heated. This allows entry of water for germination. In areas where fire is common, such as Australia (*figure 5.6*) and southern California, scarification by fire of seeds dormant in the soil ensures early recovery of certain types of vegetation after fires. This gives them an ecological advantage in that they can quickly colonise the bare soil.

Other natural ways in which scarification may be achieved include gradual attack by bacteria, or passage through the gut of a bird or other animal. The latter case also helps the dispersal of the seeds, with the added advantage that the egested waste in which the seeds are deposited is a ready-made fertiliser.

Factors affecting germination

Germination is the onset of growth of the embryo in a seed, usually after a period of dormancy. The effects of plant growth regulators and the

Box 5A An investigation of environmental factors affecting germination

Certain environmental conditions are required for germination, including the presence of water and oxygen, and the correct temperature. *Figure 5.7* shows a range of experimental test tubes which can be used to demonstrate the need for each of these, using mustard or cress seeds. These are small enough to germinate in test tubes on a support of cotton wool.

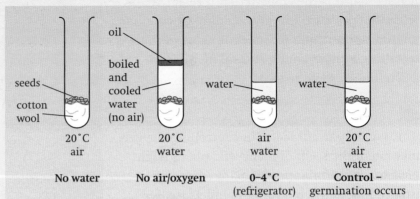

Replication: Use more than 1 seed per tube. 30 shared between several tubes for each condition should be ideal.

Quantify: More quantitative results could be obtained by calculating % germination. A range of temperatures could be attempted, if incubator facilities are available, and the optimum temperature found graphically.

● **Figure 5.7** Experiment to investigate environmental factors affecting germination of cress seeds.

Box 5B An investigation of the effects of abscisic acid, kinetin and light on the breaking of dormancy

Abscisic acid (ABA) is a natural growth inhibitor which interacts with other growth regulators. Kinetin is a synthetic cytokinin, one of the three groups of growth regulators in plants that stimulate growth.

Some seeds, such as some varieties of lettuce, need light for germination. This is a phytochrome-controlled response and red light is most effective. Using seeds of a light-sensitive variety of lettuce, such as Dandie or Kloek, or simply a range of seeds, and solutions of ABA and kinetin of appropriate concentration, an experiment can be set up to investigate the effects of ABA, kinetin and white light on germination. Most seeds can be conveniently germinated on filter paper inside petri dishes.

The following experimental dishes could be set up:
- A ABA present
- B kinetin present
- C kinetin + ABA present
- D water (as a control)

These could be left in white light. A second set of four dishes could be set up and left in the dark. Addition of 50 seeds per dish would be appropriate, after soaking the filter papers in 5 cm³ of the appropriate solution and removing any air bubbles. The dishes should be incubated at 25 °C and percentage germination recorded in each dish after 2–4 days. Final concentrations of growth regulators in the dishes should be ABA 1 ppm (part per million) (1 g per million g water, or 1 mg per dm³), and kinetin 10 ppm. A convenient way of doing this is to prepare stock solutions of ABA 2 ppm and kinetin 20 ppm and to add the appropriate solution or water to the dishes as follows:
- A 2.5 cm³ ABA + 2.5 cm³ water
- B 2.5 cm³ kinetin + 2.5 cm³ water
- C 2.5 cm³ kinetin + 2.5 cm³ ABA
- D 5 cm³ water

environment on germination can be investigated experimentally. *Boxes 5A, 5B* and *5C* describe investigations that can be carried out into the roles of environmental factors and growth regulators on germination and dormancy.

The physiology of germination

Having looked at environmental and hormonal influences on dormancy and germination, we can now summarise how these factors interact. In *box 5A* it is established that water, oxygen and a suitable temperature are required for germination.

Germination is initiated by the uptake of water, a process known as **imbibition**, which takes place through the micropyle and testa. As the contents of the seed hydrate, they swell and rupture the testa (and pericarp if necessary), allowing the radicle and plumule to emerge (*figure 3.17*). Water has several vital functions. It is an essential

Box 5C An investigation into the role of gibberellins in breaking dormancy of cereal seeds

As we have seen, gibberellins are one of the three classes of growth regulator that promote growth. One of their effects is to break the dormancy of cereal seeds. This is achieved by stimulation of enzymes that hydrolyse (digest) the food reserves in the endosperm. In particular, activity of the enzyme α-amylase is stimulated, which catalyses starch digestion (*Biology 2*, chapter 6).

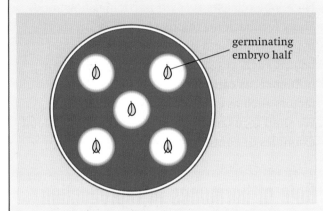

germinating
embryo half

● **Figure 5.8** Final appearance of petri dishes.

SAQ 5.12

The following experiment was set up to demonstrate production of α-amylase by germinating barley. Five barley grains were cut in half so that in each case one half contained the embryo and the other just endosperm. The 'non-embryo halves' were discarded. The 'embryo halves' were surface sterilised (bacterial and fungal contaminants can also produce α-amylase) and placed in a petri dish containing sterilised starch-agar medium (agar jelly containing starch). They were incubated at 25 °C for 48 hours. The surface of the starch agar was then flooded with iodine solution. The final appearance of the dish is shown in *figure 5.8*. The 'halos' around each grain are due to the digestion of starch by α-amylase which has diffused out of the grain. In the rest of the agar, iodine solution has reacted with starch to give a blue-black colour. How could you gain evidence to support the hypothesis that the production of α-amylase is dependent on gibberellin produced in the embryo?

---

solvent, allowing biochemical reactions to take place in solution, and the transport of nutrients from the food reserves to the growing embryo. It is also a reagent, taking part in the many hydrolysis (digestive) reactions by which the food stored in the cotyledons or the endosperm is broken down. Overall, therefore, water activates the seed.

Oxygen is needed for aerobic respiration. The respiratory substrates, mainly glucose and lipids (usually oils), come from the food reserves. The resulting release of carbon dioxide is responsible for an initial loss in total dry mass of the seed (see SAQ 1.9). If there is an oxygen shortage, seeds can also respire anaerobically, producing ethanol and carbon dioxide from glucose.

Since the biochemical reactions of germination are controlled by enzymes, temperature affects the rate at which they act. There will be an optimum temperature for germination and a range outside which germination will not occur.

During the early phases of germination, mobilisation of the food reserves takes place. This is controlled by regulators such as gibberellins, abscisic acid, cytokinins and auxins, as investigated in *boxes 5B* and *5C*. The role of gibberellins in cereal seeds is a good example (*box 5C* and SAQ 5.12). Here gibberellins are produced by the embryo at the onset of germination and stimulate the synthesis of new, key enzymes. This involves switching on the relevant genes which code for the enzymes. Similar events occur in all germinating seeds. One role for these enzymes is to hydrolyse (digest) the food reserves. Carbohydrates (such as starch), lipids and proteins are hydrolysed to sugars, fatty acids and glycerol, and amino acids, respectively. These products are used by the growing embryo, together with the minerals and vitamins also stored, as building blocks for new biochemicals, or as respiratory substrates. For example, as cells divide, new cell walls must be made, using glucose to make cellulose, as described in *Biology 1*, chapter 2. Amino acids are needed to synthesise new proteins, including enzymes and structural proteins. In the embryo, cell division takes place in the apical meristem of the root (the radicle) and the apical meristem of the shoot (the plumule). Zones of enlargement and differentiation occur behind the meristem as described in chapter 1 on pages 4 and 5.

Hormonal control in animals

As noted at the beginning of this chapter, the chemical control of growth, development and reproduction in animals is brought about by hormones. Hormones have been studied in chapter 6 of *Biology 2* and we looked at some examples in chapter 4 here. They may be defined as chemical messengers. The term 'messenger' is used because they always travel from their site of synthesis to their site of action (the 'target') in the blood. Hormones work with the nervous system to bring about control and co-ordination. Each hormone has a specific target or targets. This specificity occurs because particular receptor sites exist at the target cells, either in the plasma membranes or the cytoplasm.

All animal hormones have the following characteristics:

- chemical messengers;
- small molecules;
- made in endocrine glands;
- travel in blood;
- effective in small concentrations;
- have specific targets.

The hypothalamus and pituitary gland

In humans, all aspects of sexual reproduction, including puberty, pregnancy, birth, lactation and menopause are orchestrated by hormones. We have already seen that the hypothalamus and pituitary gland are the major control centres for these hormones (*figures 5.9, 4.13, 4.14 and 4.15*). This is also true for growth and development. The hypothalamus is a link between the endocrine system and the

nervous system. It is a relatively small though complicated structure lying at the base of the brain. It receives information from other parts of the brain and from the blood flowing through it and regulates the activity of the pituitary gland, an endocrine gland which in turn regulates other endocrine glands. Hence the pituitary gland is sometimes known as the 'master gland'. It is about the size of a pea and hangs down from the hypothalamus on a short stalk (*figure 5.9*). It has two main parts, the anterior and posterior lobes. Each lobe releases its own particular hormones. Many feedback mechanisms operate on the hypothalamus and pituitary. Environmental factors such as seasonal changes can have an influence, as can psychological and physical factors such as emotions, stress and exercise. We shall focus on some of the better understood examples of control and coordination.

Role of hormones in reproduction

The vital role that hormones play in helping to control reproduction has already been seen in chapter 4, where spermatogenesis, the menstrual cycle and pregnancy were discussed. In this section we shall look at further ways in which hormones are involved in reproduction (summarised in *table 5.2*).

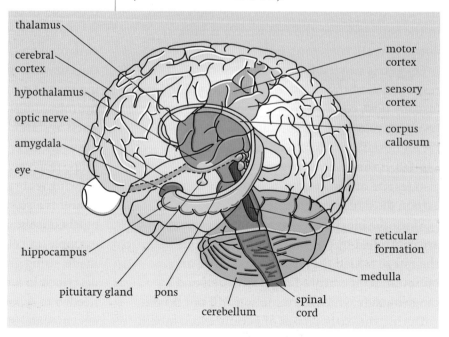

● **Figure 5.9** Location of the pituitary gland and hypothalamus in the brain.

Hormone	Site of production	Targets	Effects
Menstrual cycle			
FSH (follicle stimulating hormone)	anterior pituitary gland	ovary	development of primary follicle
oestrogen	ovary (theca layer of follicles)	anterior pituitary gland and hypothalamus	stimulates release of FSH and LH at high levels and inhibits their release at low levels
		uterus	stimulates growth
LH (luteinising hormone)	anterior pituitary gland	ovary	causes ovulation; stimulates remains of ovarian follicle to develop into corpus luteum; stimulates release of progesterone; reduces oestrogen production
progesterone	ovary (corpus luteum)	anterior pituitary gland and hypothalamus	inhibits FSH and LH
		uterus	stimulates growth and glandular activity
		cervix	suppresses penetration of sperm through cervical mucus
Pregnancy			
CG (chorionic gonadotrophin)	chorion/placenta	ovary	signal that woman is pregnant; maintains corpus luteum for about the first 3 months of pregnancy
oestrogen	corpus luteum, then placenta	anterior pituitary gland and hypothalamus	inhibits FSH and LH; inhibits release of prolactin (and therefore inhibits lactation)
		uterus	stimulates growth; increases sensitivity to oxytocin
		breasts	stimulates development of duct system
progesterone	corpus luteum, then placenta	anterior pituitary gland and hypothalamus	inhibits FSH and LH; inhibits release of prolactin
		uterus	stimulates growth and glandular activity; decreases sensitivity to oxytocin (relaxes muscle)
		breasts	stimulates development of milk glands
HPL (human placental lactogen)	placenta	whole body	modifies glucose and fat metabolism of mother in favour of baby
Birth			
oxytocin	hypothalamus, but released from posterior pituitary gland	uterus	contraction of muscle, causing labour
Lactation			
HPL	placenta	breasts	stimulates growth and development
		whole body	modifies glucose and fat metabolism of mother in favour of baby
PRF (prolactin releasing factor)	hypothalamus	anterior pituitary gland	release of prolactin
prolactin	anterior pituitary gland	breasts	stimulates glandular cells to produce milk
oxytocin	hypothalamus, but released from posterior pituitary gland	breasts	ejaculation of milk during breast feeding

● **Table 5.2** Summary of the role of hormones in the female in human sexual reproduction.

Role of hormones in birth

Towards the end of pregnancy, an as yet unknown signal, probably from the fetus itself, triggers the events which lead to labour and birth. The muscle layer of the uterus becomes increasingly sensitive to the hormone **oxytocin**, due to a decline in progesterone levels. Oxytocin is made in the hypothalamus and passes down special nerve cells to be released from the posterior lobe of the pituitary gland. Its target is the uterus, where it causes muscle contractions. There now occurs a rare example of **positive feedback** (most feedback mechanisms are negative). Uterine contractions stimulate release of more oxytocin via nerve connections with the hypothalamus. Oxytocin in turn stimulates more contractions. Thus during labour, contractions get more frequent and more powerful. The contractions force the fetus through the cervix and into the vagina from where it emerges to the outside world. Further contractions result in the delivery of the placenta or 'afterbirth'.

Role of hormones in lactation

Lactation is the production of milk by the breasts. The breasts grow and develop during pregnancy (on average doubling in weight). Oestrogen and progesterone help to control this development, as shown in *figure 4.23*. They can only have this effect in the presence of **human placental lactogen (HPL)**. Milk, however, can only be produced in the presence of **prolactin**, a polypeptide hormone secreted by the anterior lobe of the pituitary gland in response to **prolactin releasing factor (PRF)** from the hypothalamus. Prolactin levels build up during pregnancy, but high levels of oestrogen and progesterone, secreted by the placenta, restrict its release and therefore prevent milk production. At birth, loss of the placenta results in a lot more prolactin being released by the pituitary as the oestrogen and progesterone are no longer secreted. Its target is the breasts, where it stimulates the glandular cells that produce milk (*figure 5.10*). These cells are surrounded by contractile tissue, which squeezes the milk into ducts leading to the nipples. Oxytocin (made in the hypothalamus and released from the posterior pituitary gland) stimulates contraction of this tissue. The sucking of the baby on the breast sets up a nervous reflex which stimulates the hypothalamus to

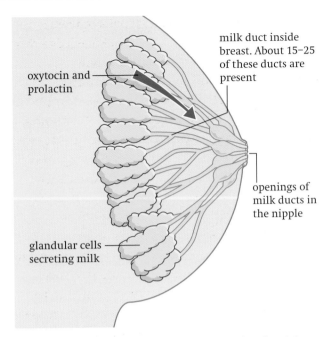

* **Figure 5.10** Female breast showing glands with milk ducts opening in the nipple.

release more oxytocin and maintain milk flow. Another reflex to the hypothalamus stimulates the release of prolactin releasing factor, which stimulates prolactin release from the pituitary. Thus, oxytocin stimulates milk ejection and prolactin stimulates milk production. Both hormones depend on suckling for their continued synthesis. If the baby does not suckle frequently, milk production drops.

SAQ 5.13

Describe the broad overall changes in concentration that you would expect for the following hormones in the mother's blood during pregnancy and lactation: **a** progesterone from the corpus luteum; **b** progesterone from the placenta; **c** prolactin; **d** oxytocin; **e** HPL; **f** HCG. You will also need to refer back to chapter 4 to answer this.

Role of hormones in premenstrual tension

The term **premenstrual tension (PMT)** was first used in 1931 to describe the 'distressing psychological or physical symptoms' which some women experience regularly towards the end of each menstrual cycle and which 'significantly regress throughout the rest of the cycle'. Tension is not the only symptom. In fact, more than 150 symptoms have been attributed to PMT at various times, and the term **premenstrual syndrome** (**PMS**) was introduced in 1953 to acknowledge this variety of effects. Great controversy now surrounds the condition. In 1993, certain psychologists (not all of them men) went so far as to suggest that it may not exist at all, that it was more of a 'social construct' than a medical condition, and that it was a way of 'legitimising and expressing distress'. However, some women who experience it describe the condition as devastating and about 75% of women are said to be affected in some way. The most common symptoms are depression, changes in mood, water retention and aches and pains. Little is known about the cause, but it is usually assumed to be hormonal in origin. Since it takes place in the few days before menstruation, it could be due to changes in the balance between progesterone and oestrogen (*figure 4.15*), which decline at different rates at this time. Dr Katharine Dalton, who coined the term PMS, believes it may commonly be due to progesterone deficiency.

Menopause and hormone replacement therapy

Menopause is the cessation of monthly periods and marks the end of a woman's fertility. The average age of menopause in the UK is 51 years. Periods usually become irregular, before finally ceasing. The cause is the gradual failure of the ovaries. The number of follicles declines and they become less sensitive to FSH so that eggs are less and less likely to be produced each month. This means that the secretion of oestrogen declines and, since oestrogen normally inhibits FSH by negative feedback, higher levels of FSH (and later LH) are typical of menopause. Many symptoms, both physical and psychological, are associated with menopause and these are mostly due to the reduced oestrogen levels (although progesterone levels also decline). The commonest symptoms are night sweats, random hot flushes during the day, and vaginal dryness. Other common symptoms are depression, irritability, fatigue, and a gradual softening of the bones. This latter is due to loss of minerals, particularly calcium and creates a condition known as **osteoporosis**. It is characterised by loss of bone mass; as a result the bones break more easily. It occurs because oestrogen is

antagonistic to the hormone **parathormone**, which stimulates the raising of blood calcium levels, drawing the calcium from the bones. Most of the symptoms of menopause can be prevented relatively easily by **hormone replacement therapy** (**HRT**), in which oestrogen is taken either in pill form or by implants below the skin. For instance, HRT greatly reduces the rate at which calcium is lost from the bones, slowing it down to roughly the same rate as in men. Treatment with HRT can be short-term or continued for years, although in the long term, blood clotting and other undesirable side effects may occur. Some of these can be prevented by adding progesterone to the oestrogen.

Role of hormones in growth and development

Growth hormone

The anterior lobe of the pituitary gland produces a hormone called **growth hormone** (**GH**). It has no specific target organ, but regulates the growth of all parts of the body. It does this by stimulating protein synthesis. It is particularly important for development of limb bones and skeletal muscle. Thus an excess of growth hormone results in gigantism and a deficiency results in dwarfism, although brain development and IQ are unaffected. GH also increases the rate of cell growth and cell division and favours the use of fat rather than carbohydrate for energy so the body becomes less fat and more muscular. Secretion of GH itself is under the control of the hypothalamus, with both a stimulating hormone and an inhibitory hormone being involved. Feedback inhibition from GH appears not to occur.

Secondary sexual characteristics

At the beginning of puberty, the hypothalamus begins to release **gonadotrophin releasing hormone** (**GnRH**), which stimulates the secretion of FSH and LH from the pituitary gland. These in turn stimulate the testes to produce testosterone, or the ovaries to produce oestrogen. These hormones are responsible for the development of **secondary sexual characteristics** such as pubic hair and enlarged genital organs.

The thyroid gland

The thyroid gland secretes two hormones which influence growth and development by affecting the rate of metabolic activity. These hormones are **thyroxine (tetra-iodothyronine** or **T$_4$)** and **tri-iodothyronine** (or **T$_3$**). The numbers refer to the number of iodine atoms per molecule. About 90% of the secretion is of thyroxine, and the two hormones act in a similar way, so we shall only consider thyroxine in the following account.

The thyroid gland has two lobes and is arranged like a bow tie around the front of the trachea in the neck. *Figure 5.11* shows the structure of the gland. It is made up of many follicles, each of which is a hollow sphere surrounded by a single layer of secretory cells (epithelium). These cells secrete a glycoprotein called **thyroglobulin**, which accumulates in the follicles. Thyroglobulin is a large molecule, containing iodine.

When thyroxine is to be released into the bloodstream, the secretory cells take up small amounts of the stored thyroglobulin from the follicles by

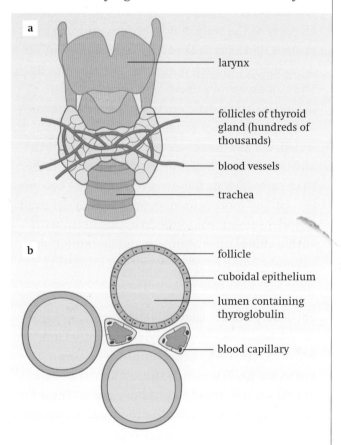

● **Figure 5.11** Structure of the thyroid gland.
a Position in the neck.
b Transverse section showing three follicles.

pinocytosis. Inside the pinocytotic vesicles, enzymes hydrolyse the large thyroglobulin molecules into smaller thyroxine molecules. These then travel through the cell, and pass into the blood capillaries.

Thyroxine is a small molecule carried in solution in the blood plasma, attached to plasma proteins. Once released from these proteins, the thyroxine enters cells throughout the body.

Role of thyroxine in growth and development

Thyroxine controls **basal metabolic rate (BMR)**. Metabolism is the collective name for all the chemical processes going on in the body. The basal rate is the rate at rest. It is the rate at which oxygen and energy-containing nutrients are used to release energy, and is directly related to the rate of cell respiration. When thyroxine enters cells, it binds to specific protein receptor molecules in the cell nucleus. The combined thyroxine–receptor complex attaches to specific regions of DNA and 'switches on' transcription of mRNA, thus bringing about synthesis of whatever protein is coded for by that particular piece of DNA. Many different genes are transcribed, leading to the production of a wide variety of enzymes. This increases the metabolic rate of the cell. The rate of respiration, in particular, increases.

Thyroxine influences growth and development in a number of ways. It stimulates growth in general, but particularly protein synthesis and development of the skeletal system. Unlike growth hormone (GH), it also stimulates brain development, so a thyroxine deficiency in children can result not only in dwarfism, but mental retardation and low IQ (cretinism).

Thyroid deficiency is known as **hypothyroidism**. A condition called **myxoedema** may result in which a lowered metabolic rate brings decreased respiration, breathing and heart rates; a lower body temperature; reduced mental alertness; slower and poorly coordinated movements; and increased weight, despite a reduced appetite. Sufferers also sleep for long periods but with little benefit. A characteristic puffiness of the face and husky voice along with very dry skin and hair loss may also occur. A serious deficiency that goes untreated can eventually cause coma. Replacement thyroxine taken in tablet form restores and maintains normal growth and development in both children and adults but this treatment must be continued daily for life.

An *over*active thyroid (**hyperthyroidism**) results in a high metabolic rate with an associated increase in respiration, breathing and heart rates and a higher body temperature. Sufferers rarely stay still – they find it hard to sleep – and are quick in their movements. They can become agitated, nervous and irritable, and will lose weight, despite eating more. They may even experience heart palpitations. Treatment is normally by a short course of drugs or radioactive iodine that partially destroy the thyroid gland. If that is not appropriate or successful, part of the gland can be surgically removed. Both of these treatments are difficult to judge accurately and may result in too *low* a level of thyroxine. However, this can be compensated for by taking replacement thyroxine tablets as above.

Circulating in the blood, the hormone is bound tightly to the plasma proteins that carry it, so it is released only slowly over days or weeks. Once it has entered its target cells, it gradually switches on genes, and so the basal metabolic rate only changes very gradually over weeks or maybe even months. This can make treatment difficult to 'tune' if someone has an overactive or underactive thyroid gland.

Control of thyroxine secretion

The control of thyroxine secretion is summarised in *figure 5.12*. A straightforward negative feedback system operates, again involving the pituitary gland and hypothalamus, as well as two other hormones. The hypothalamus secretes **thyrotrophin releasing hormone (TRH)** which passes directly along a blood vessel to the anterior lobe of the pituitary gland. In response to this hormone, the anterior pituitary gland secretes **thyroid stimulating hormone (TSH)** into the blood. TSH is carried in the blood to the thyroid gland, where it stimulates the secretion of thyroxine.

High levels of thyroxine in the blood reduce the secretion of both TRH and TSH and thus, in time, thyroxine levels will fall again. As well as this negative feedback system, higher centres of the brain may also be involved, which may in turn respond to environmental cues. For example, the basal metabolic rate may be increased during cold seasons to help maintain body temperature.

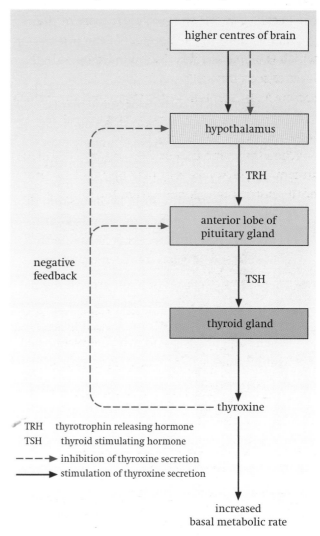

● **Figure 5.12** Control of thyroxine secretion.

SUMMARY

◆ Internal coordination and control of growth and development are genetically programmed. In plants this is achieved entirely by chemicals. These chemicals are referred to as growth regulators or growth substances. In animals both chemicals and the nervous system are involved and the chemicals are referred to as hormones.

◆ In both plants and animals the environment also has an important influence on growth and development. These processes can therefore be seen to be a product of the interaction between genes and the environment.

◆ Flowering is often controlled by day length (photoperiod). In such cases, some plants flower in response to short days (short-day plants) and some in response to long days (long-day plants). The blue-green pigment phytochrome is responsible for this. It is converted to an active form by absorption of red light; far-red light or an extended dark period reverses this process. A hormone that controls flowering has not been found.

◆ There are five classes of plant growth regulators, namely auxins, gibberellins and cytokinins, which are growth promoters, and ethene and abscisic acid, which are regarded as inhibitors.

◆ Flowering, fruit maturation, dormancy and germination are good examples of the interaction between environment and growth regulators in plants.

◆ All the growth promoters are involved in fruit growth, particularly auxins. Fruit ripening is often stimulated by ethene.

◆ Germination requires particular environmental conditions, including water, oxygen and a suitable temperature. It can only occur once seed dormancy is broken.

◆ Seed dormancy is often caused by growth inhibitors, and broken by growth promoters. Gibberellins break dormancy in cereal seeds. Dormancy is sometimes broken by environmental factors such as light or an extended cold season.

◆ In humans, the process of labour and birth is stimulated by oxytocin, a hormone produced by the hypothalamus and released from the posterior lobe of the pituitary. Oxytocin stimulates contraction of muscle in the uterus wall. Its secretion is regulated by positive feedback.

◆ Premenstrual tension is probably hormonal in origin and may be due to changes in the balance between oestrogen and progesterone towards the end of the menstrual cycle.

◆ The menopause is caused by failing ovaries, which leads to a decline in oestrogen levels. The undesirable consequences, such as a greater risk of osteoporosis, can be avoided by hormone replacement therapy. This involves giving oestrogen pills or implants.

◆ The hypothalamus and pituitary gland influence growth and development as well as reproduction. The anterior lobe of the pituitary, under the influence of the hypothalamus, secretes growth hormone which stimulates protein synthesis and the development of limb bones.

◆ Development of secondary sexual characteristics is triggered once the hypothalamus releases gonadotrophin releasing hormone (GnRH).

◆ The thyroid gland secretes thyroxine, which controls basal metabolic rate and thereby influences growth and development. Limb growth and brain development are particularly affected in the fetus or child and many aspects of day to day activity and behaviour in both children and adults.

◆ Secretion of thyroxine is stimulated by TSH (thyroid stimulating hormone) from the pituitary, which in turn is stimulated by TRH (thyrotrophin releasing hormone) from the hypothalamus. Thyroxine regulates its own production by negative feedback.

Questions

1 Describe germination in a named dicotyledonous seed. (You will need to use information from both chapters 3 and 5. A suitable example could be the broad bean, a non-endospermic seed. Some of the information in SAQ 1.9 will be useful but remember that the broad bean stores food in its cotyledons, not in its endosperm. Remember that cereals are monocotyledonous.)

2 Discuss the role of plant growth regulators in fruit and seed development.

3 What are the advantages of a period of seed dormancy to a plant species? Describe the mechanisms by which dormancy is controlled.

4 Discuss the roles of the hypothalamus and pituitary gland in controlling reproduction in
a the human male and
b the human female. (Refer also to chapter 4 where relevant.)

5 Discuss the roles of the hypothalamus and pituitary gland in controlling human growth and development.

6 a Show how hormonal regulation of the menstrual cycle and of thyroxine secretion illustrate the principles of negative feedback. (See also chapter 4.)
b Give an example of positive feedback and explain how it differs from negative feedback.

7 Discuss some of the ways in which knowledge of plant growth regulators has had important commercial applications.

8 Discuss the role of light in regulating plant flowering.

9 Discuss the importance to plants and animals of being able to respond to environmental factors, as well as genetic factors, in the regulation of their growth and development.

Answers to self-assessment questions

Chapter 1

1.1 For cells to increase in size or number, new materials must be added. (These include the common biochemicals, particularly protein.)

1.2
a According to the definition, growth is accompanied by an increase in mass, but the ball of cells is formed with no increase in mass. (The cells become smaller and smaller with each division. Increase in cell size *and* mass only occurs once a food supply becomes available).

b Also according to the definition, growth is accompanied by an *irreversible* increase in *dry* mass. If *fresh* mass is increasing, but dry mass is decreasing, the increase in mass is due to water. Increase in water content is in theory reversible under dry conditions, although perhaps unlikely to happen here.

1.3 Mitosis.

1.4 The two daughter cells are genetically identical (clones).

1.5
a 1.5 mm.
b 4 mm.
c Cell 1 was still in the zone of cell division at the start of the experiment, whereas cell 2 had just entered the zone of cell enlargement. Cell 1 was still in the zone of cell division after 5 hours when it was still only 1 mm from the tip (the zone of cell division is 2 mm). Meanwhile, new cells are being added between cell 1 and cell 2, in the zone of enlargement, increasing the distance between them. These new cells are also elongating, further increasing the distance.
d From 10 mm onwards because, as stated, the zone of cell enlargement extends from 2–10 mm from the tip. *Figure 1.2a* shows that mature xylem is found at the point where the zone of cell enlargement ends.
e Cells nearer the end of the root tip than cells 1 and 2 are dividing. This results in new cells being added to the end of the root, so the distance between cells 1 and 2 and the end of the root tip increases as the root grows longer. Once cells 1 and 2 enter the zone of cell enlargement, increases in the length of cells below them also increase the distance between these cells and the end of the tip.
f After 7.5 hours, cell 2 leaves the zone of enlargement (10 mm from the tip). The number of elongating cells between cell 2 and the tip is now at its maximum and is constant.
g The curves would be linear between 20 and 40 hours because the rate of elongation of the root would be constant.
h 2.5 mm per hour (from the steepest part of the curves).

1.6
a Growth rate of boys and girls is very similar for the first nine years after birth. The growth rate is relatively high at birth, then falls rapidly from over 24 cm per year in the first year to about 9 cm per year at the age of two years. Growth rate continues to decline, but more slowly, until the beginning of the adolescent spurt. This occurs roughly between the ages of nine and 13 in girls, and between 12 and 15 in boys. At the peak of the adolescent spurt, girls grow about 9 cm per year, and boys about 10 cm per year. After the adolescent spurt, growth rate in both sexes declines rapidly (within 2–3 years) to near zero.
b Boys. This is because boys start the adolescent spurt about 2–3 years later than girls, and will have been growing during that time. (Because girls start their adolescent spurts sooner than boys, they are often taller than boys between the ages of 9 and 13.)
c (i) The earliest age shown (about 6 months).
(ii) the same as (i).
d (i) About 9 cm per year.
(ii) About 10 cm per year.

1.7 Growth could be measured as an increase in: size (e.g. height, length, volume); dry mass or fresh mass; number of cells; complexity.

1.8 a See graph.

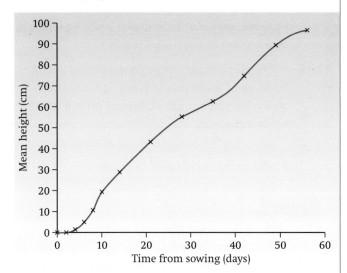

● **Answer for** SAQ 1.8

 b An absolute growth curve.
 c An absolute growth rate curve and a relative growth rate curve. (Some processing of the data would be necessary.)

1.9 a See graph.

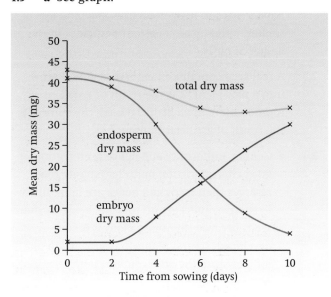

● **Answer for** SAQ 1.9a

b (i) The dry mass of the endosperm declines slightly in the first two days as germination begins, and then declines faster over the next eight days. This is because, as the seed germinates, the food in the endosperm (mainly starch) is digested by enzymes and the products of digestion move to the growing embryo.
(ii) The dry mass of the embryo increases steadily after two days. This is because the embryo is growing, using materials obtained from the endosperm. These materials include glucose obtained from the starch in the endosperm, and amino acids obtained from proteins in the endosperm.
(iii) Total dry mass declines from 43 mg to 33 mg, a drop of 23.3%, over the first eight days. This is due to loss of carbon dioxide gas as a waste product of aerobic respiration.

 c See graph.

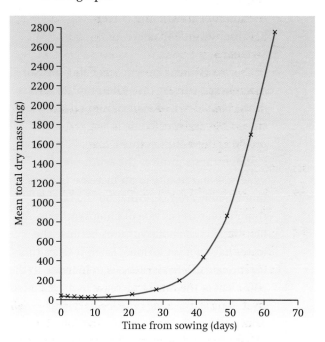

● **Answer for** SAQ 1.9b

d Dry mass increases from day 8 at an ever-increasing rate. The increase is almost exponential, with a doubling in dry mass occurring roughly every week after 14 days. The increase in dry mass is due to photosynthesis. As soon as the first leaf appears and is exposed to light, the plant is able to photosynthesise. As soon as the increase in dry mass due to photosynthesis exceeds the loss in dry mass due to respiration, the plant shows a net increase in dry mass. (Note: you will gain a better understanding of these changes when you study germination in chapter 5. The experiment described in *box 5C* is particularly relevant.)

1.10 **a** A = rate of growth (rate declines after initial rapid increase); B = dry mass (could not be zero at Day 0 and could not be negative up to 11 days).
b Shoot length would show no initial decrease.
c A = absolute growth rate curve; B = absolute growth curve.
d Sigmoid.
e In this experiment growth was being measured as an increase in *dry* mass. Respiration results in the breakdown of materials to release energy but carbon dioxide is lost as a waste product. There is therefore a loss of dry mass. Photosynthesis involves the synthesis of materials and results in an increase in mass. Immediately after germination the rate of respiration exceeds rate of photosynthesis. At first there is *no* photosynthesis because the leaves have not yet formed. Later, it takes time for the rate of photosynthesis to increase to the point where the rate of increase in mass due to photosynthesis exceeds the losses due to respiration.

1.11 Increase in fresh mass. Increase in size of an anatomical feature, e.g. length of hind leg, length of developing wing, length of head.

1.12 Head – bears sensory structures/feeding structures. These are important throughout life and it is important they are fully developed early. Tibia – related to growth of leg; must increase in proportion to rest of body for efficient locomotion. Wings – not needed until adulthood (for migration to new food sources) and mating. Expanded wings cannot moult.

1.13 1024, that is 2 after 30 minutes, 4 after 1 hour, 8 after 1.5 hours, etc. It is a characteristic of exponential growth that the population doubles with each generation.

1.14 Bacteria are adjusting to the conditions. For example, they may have to make new enzymes in order to use the nutrients present.

1.15 Nutrients running out, oxygen running out, build up of waste products (e.g. ethanol from anaerobic respiration), change in pH (e.g. build up of lactic acid).

1.16 **a** Where the curve flattens out.
b Where the curve starts to go down.

Chapter 2

2.1 If gametes did not have half the number of chromosomes of normal body cells, the number of chromosomes would double with each generation as a result of the fusion of male and female gametes.

2.2 There are many possibilities, such as: climate change, (e.g. colder winters); increase in predators or hunting by humans; new parasites; new pathogens (infectious diseases); reduction in availability of food (due, for example, to loss of habitat such as hedgerows or woodland); loss of shelter; build-up of persistent pesticides in the bodies of birds.

2.3 A real seed contains an embryo that will grow into a new plant. It is the result of *sexual* reproduction. In an artificial seed, the embryo is the result of artificial cloning.

2.4 **a** Genetic uniformity and hence preservation of good characteristics; bulbs have larger food reserves than seeds and hence are more likely to survive; bulbs get off to a quicker start than seeds because the young plant is better developed; several plants may grow from one bulb because the bulb contains both terminal and axillary buds.
b Lack of the genetic variation found among seeds means that better variants cannot be selected; it may be cheaper or less labour intensive to sow seeds rather than bulbs.

Chapter 3

3.1

Characteristic	White deadnettle (insect pollinated)	Meadow fescue (wind pollinated)
petals	large, conspicuous nectaries present scented landing platform for bees	no petals no nectaries no scent no landing platform
stamens	inside flower stamens and anthers do not swing freely	hang outside flower to catch wind stamens and anthers swing freely in air currents
pollen	rough surfaced	light, small, smooth surfaced relatively large amount produced
stigma	inside flower sticky and lobed to trap pollen	feathery and hangs outside flower, therefore traps pollen more easily

3.2 **a** See diagram.

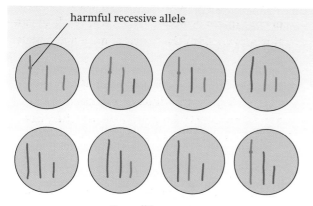

harmful recessive allele

8 possible gametes

● **Answer for** SAQ 3.2

b 64. Any one of the eight possible male gametes could fuse with any one of the eight possible female gametes; 8 × 8 = 64.

c 50% / half / 4 out of 8.

d 25% / quarter (half x half).

e None. The cross here is between a heterozygous parent and a homozygous normal plant. In such a cross, half the offspring would be homozygous normal and half would be heterozygous (one copy of the normal allele and one copy of the harmful allele). Heterozygous individuals would be carriers of the harmful allele, but be phenotypically normal because the harmful allele is recessive.

f Crossing over in meiosis I, and random mutation.

g All the diploid cells of a given plant are genetically identical since they are all derived from the original zygote by mitosis. This includes the tissues of the flowers. Genetic variation only arises once meiosis takes place. Thus, just as much variation can exist among the gametes produced by one flower as between gametes from different flowers.

h Self-pollination leads to self-fertilisation. Four processes occur which can lead to genetic variation in the offspring. These are independent assortment of chromosomes and crossing over in meiosis I, random fusion of gametes and random mutation in the gametes. Self-fertilisation increases greatly the chances of harmful recessive alleles pairing up to produce homozygous individuals suffering from the harmful condition.

Asexual reproduction results in no genetic variation among the offspring.

Cross-pollination results in much greater variation than self-pollination.

3.3 **a** Stigma above anthers = pin-eyed;
stigma below anthers = thrum-eyed.

  b Pollen deposited on the body of the bee while
it feeds in the tube of one flower tends to pass
to the stigma at the same level in another
flower.

3.4 The *tube nucleus* controls growth of the pollen
tube. The *generative nucleus* divides by mitosis to
form the two male gametes.

3.5 It is an adaptation to life on land. Fertilisation is
dependent on water if swimming sperm are
released from the plant. Pollen grains, with their
protective waterproof outer walls, are ideally
suited for transport in dry conditions.

3.6 Vacuoles almost disappear since these are the
sites of most water within plant cells. Food stores
increase, for example oils and starch.

3.7 During meiosis of a triploid nucleus, homo-
logous chromosomes come together in threes
(trivalents) on the spindle rather than in pairs as
in diploid cells. Organised separation of the
chromosomes to opposite ends of the spindle is
impossible since two of each trivalent must go
one way, and one the other.

  The endosperm nuclei never divide by meiosis.
No other cells are derived from the endosperm.
Ultimately they all die within the seed, being
used only as a source of food.

Chapter 4

4.1 **a** (i) 4   (ii) 2.

  b Spermatid.

4.2 Similarity: haploid.
Differences:

Egg	Sperm
relatively large – stores nutrients to survive early stages of development after fertilisation (it also divides into smaller cells at this stage)	relatively small – economy of material and energy
contains food store	no food store – short-lived
stationary	motile – must travel to reach egg so possesses a flagellum and a middle piece with mitochondria to provide energy for swimming
only one produced at a time – multiple pregnancy avoided (usually)	millions produced – large wastage
produced in cycles	produced continuously
many small lysosomes (cortical granules)	one large lysosome (the acrosome)

4.3 **a** Temperature varies slightly during the day,
usually rising to a peak in the afternoon and
declining at night.

  b Illness often causes a rise in temperature
which could be confused with ovulation.

  c (i) 36.7 °C
(ii) 37–37.1 °C

  d Temperature stays 'high' due to maintained
levels of progesterone.

  e 1st or 2nd of January.

4.4 This is largely due to the decline of oestrogen
levels. LH and FSH secretion can be brought back
to pre-surgery/premenopausal levels by treatment
with low levels of oestrogen (HRT).

4.5 **a** Enzymes from lysosomes in the secondary
oocyte cause the zona pellucida to thicken and
separate from the oocyte. The zona forms an
impenetrable barrier to sperm.

  b If an extra sperm fertilised the egg, three sets
of chromosomes (triploidy) would occur. This
results in early spontaneous abortion
(miscarriage). Fertilisation by several extra
sperm would cause polyploidy, also fatal.

  c Large wastage is inevitable. For example, sperm
may be defective, be killed by acid conditions
in the vagina, be unable to penetrate the

cervical mucus, or may swim up the wrong oviduct. It is estimated that only about 100 sperm survive to reach each oviduct from the 300 million released at ejaculation.

4.6 The corpus luteum is the main source of oestrogen and progesterone (until the placenta takes over this function three months into pregnancy). Both hormones are essential for maintaining the lining of the uterus and for other functions.

4.7 An excess of testosterone could act by negative feedback in the pituitary gland, blocking the action of FSH and LH and thus switching off its own production (*figure 4.13*). The excess would also prevent the normal function of testosterone of switching *on* spermatogenesis in the seminiferous tubules.

4.8 Progesterone inhibits release of GnRH by the hypothalamus in the male, as in the female. This in turn reduces production of LH, FSH and testosterone. Note, lack of testosterone reduces secondary male characteristics, so use of progesterone requires replacement of testosterone at the same time. It will probably be easier to use a testosterone-based contraceptive (SAQ 4.7).

4.9 a
- The fact that the male pill makes a man temporarily sterile may threaten the male ego and make men unlikely to use the pill. (Evidence suggests that this will probably not be a major problem.)
- Fear of being sued if harmful side-effects occur.
- The consequences of failed contraception affect mainly women, so there is always likely to be more demand for female contraception. Women may not trust men even if the man claims to be 'on the pill'.
- Side-effects could be a problem. At present there are short-term side-effects such as increased acne, oily skin and weight gain; it can take 4–6 months after stopping the pill for fertility to return; there is concern that long-term side-effects might include heart disease and prostate disease.

b
- Profit.
- The only other effective contraception for men is the condom and vasectomy.
- To give greater opportunity to men to share the responsibility for contraception.

- A spin-off from research could be a better understanding of male infertility.
- In some cultures women may find it difficult to use contraception for religious or social reasons.

4.10 It prevents implantation rather than fertilisation. RU486 works in this way.

4.11 Difficulty of separation at birth; blood groups of mother and fetus may be incompatible; to prevent the passage of bacteria from mother to fetus; harmful antigen–antibody reponses could occur.

4.12 a Chorion, chorionic villi, blood vessels from the umbilical arteries and vein.
  b Endometrium, maternal vein and artery.

4.13 a Oxygen, carbon dioxide, sodium and potassium ions, urea, fatty acids.
  b Sodium, potassium, calcium and phosphate ions, amino acids, iron, vitamins.
  c Glucose.
  d Water only.
  e Possibly fatty acids and antibodies.

4.14 a Energy in the form of carbohydrate or fat; protein; vitamins A, B_1, B_2, B_3, C; folate.
  b Protein; vitamins A, B_2, C, folate.
  c Calcium, iron, possibly vitamin D.
  d Consult *table 4.3*.

4.15 a 20–24. (Many people assume the greatest number occurs among teenagers.)
  b

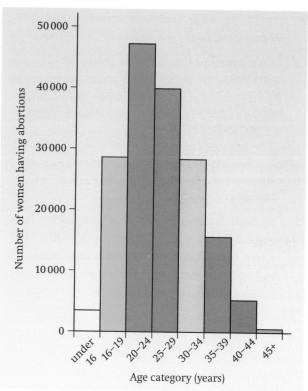

c Total number of women who had abortions
   = 167 916

under 16	2%
16–19	17%
20–24	28%
25–29	23%
30–34	17%
35–39	10%
40–44	3%
45+	0.3%
age not stated	0.008%

4.16 Capacitation must take place first.

Chapter 5

5.1 Day length varies with season, so being sensitive to day length is one way in which a plant can 'know' what time of year it is.

5.2 Temperature.

5.3 Under laboratory conditions, plants could be given short days followed by short nights. SDPs would not flower, but LDPs would. The reverse would be true for long days followed by long nights.

5.4 An absorption spectrum is a graph which shows the relative amounts of light of different wavelengths absorbed by a chemical. An action spectrum is a graph showing the relative effectiveness of different wavelengths of light in bringing about a reaction, such as flowering or photosynthesis.

5.5 Several methods are possible. Leaves could be covered to give them short days while the rest of the plant is exposed to long days. This causes flowering in a SDP. If leaves are exposed to long days while the rest of the plant receives short days, flowering does not occur.

5.6 The seeds would only germinate when water was available.

5.7 If a seed that requires light for germination is covered by soil it will not germinate. Similarly, if a seed that is inhibited by light is *not* covered, it will not germinate. Breeding out such sensitivity increases percentage germination.

5.8 If seeds with small food reserves are buried in soil, they may have insufficient food reserves to grow to the surface of the soil when they germinate. By being near the surface when germination starts, photosynthesis will start sooner.

5.9 It ensures that the seed does not germinate until it is covered by soil or dead vegetation, when it is more likely to have water and inorganic nutrients.

5.10 Seeds under a vegetation canopy, such as in woodlands and forests, will be prevented from germinating until a break in the canopy allows sunlight through for photosynthesis. Also seeds are more likely to germinate in spring when deciduous trees still have no leaves, rather than in the summer or autumn, giving the plants a longer growing season.

5.11 Phytochrome.

5.12 Set up two petri dishes. In one, use starch-agar with non-endosperm halves. No digestion of starch should take place. In the second, add gibberellin to the starch-agar and use non-embryo halves. Digestion of starch should take place around the non-embryo halves.

5.13 **a** Progesterone from the corpus luteum – initial rise, level, then decline to zero at about 3 months of pregnancy.
   b Progesterone from the placenta – starts to rise as placenta develops (from about 5 weeks) and continues to rise until birth, when it drops to zero.
   c Prolactin – rises sharply after birth. (In fact it starts to rise just before birth, from about 30 weeks of pregnancy.)
   d Oxytocin – rises sharply from just before birth to a peak at birth and then declines to a low level just after birth. Some is produced during lactation.
   e HPL – gradually increases during pregnancy.
   f HCG – rises from time of implantation and then declines from 3 months.

Glossary

abscisic acid a plant **growth regulator** that acts as an inhibitor, e.g. it is responsible for **dormancy** of some seeds and buds.

absolute growth (*or* **actual growth**) increase in size or mass.

absolute growth rate the amount of **absolute growth** in a given time period, e.g. an increase in height of 2 cm per year.

acrosome a large lysosome found in the **sperm** head.

acrosome reaction the process during which the **acrosome** swells and releases its enzymes just before **fertilisation**. The enzymes help digest a path to the **egg**.

amniocentesis the removal of a sample of **amniotic fluid** by means of a hollow needle inserted through the wall of the abdomen. Testing and examination of the fluid and of the fetal cells it contains allows prenatal diagnosis of certain disorders.

amnion a sac-like structure which grows from the **embryo**. The embryo or **fetus** is suspended inside.

amniotic cavity the space inside the **amnion**.

amniotic fluid fluid inside the **amniotic cavity**, that protects the **embryo** or **fetus** from physical damage.

androecium the male reproductive parts of a flower, consisting of a collection of **stamens**.

anther the part of a flower which produces **pollen** in pollen sacs. When the pollen is ripe the anther splits (dehisces) to release it.

asexual reproduction the production of new individuals from a single parent without the production of **gametes**. *See also* **cloning**.

auxins a class of plant **growth regulator** that generally stimulate **growth**.

binary fission a form of **asexual reproduction** in which a cell divides into two identical cells.

callus a mass of disorganised and unspecialised plant cells often produced in **micropropagation**.

capacitation the process that freshly ejaculated **sperm** must undergo before they can fertilise an **egg**. It involves the removal of a layer of glycoproteins and proteins from the outer surface of the sperm.

carpel the basic unit of the female part of a flower. It consists of a **stigma**, **style** and **ovary**. Flowers contain from one to many carpels which may be separate or fused together.

chorionic gonadotrophin (CG) a hormone produced by the **embryo** that acts as a signal that the woman is pregnant. This prevents degeneration of the **corpus luteum**.

cloning asexual reproduction. All the individuals produced by one parent are genetically identical **clones**. Artificial cloning of plants and animals is becoming increasingly common, important and, in some cases, controversial.

corpus luteum a structure that develops from an ovarian **follicle** after **ovulation**. It secretes **oestrogen** and **progesterone** which help prepare the **uterus** for **implantation**.

cotyledon (*or* **seed leaf**) the first leaf of a plant **embryo** which is very simple in structure. *See also* **monocotyledons** and **dicotyledons**.

Cowper's glands a pair of glands in the male reproductive system that contribute fluid to the **semen**.

cytokinins a class of plant **growth regulator** that stimulate cell division. They can be used to stimulate shoot **growth** in **tissue cultures**.

development a progressive series of changes that includes the specialisation of cells. *See also* **differentiation**.

dicotyledon a flowering plant that has two **cotyledons** in its **seeds**.

differentiation the process of specialisation of cells, e.g. a cell from an apical **meristem** differentiating into an epidermal cell.

dioecious a plant that produces separate male and female plants, e.g. the willow. **Self-pollination** is therefore impossible.

dormancy the state in which **seed** germination will not occur.

egg commonly used to refer to the female **gamete**. Strictly speaking, the egg is formed from the secondary **oocyte** by meiosis II.

embryo a very young stage of an organism that develops from the **zygote** before birth in animals or germination in plants. *See also* **fetus**.

embryo sac the region in a flower where the **embryo** and **endosperm** are formed and develop. It develops in the **ovule** from a single haploid cell produced by meiosis.

endosperm a triploid tissue found in **seeds** which either develops into a food store in **endospermous seeds**, or breaks down in **non-endospermous seeds** where the **cotyledons** store food.

endometrium the lining of the **uterus** which is rich in blood vessels and glands. It breaks down and is shed during **menstruation**, but helps to form the **placenta** during pregnancy.

epididymis a coiled tube, about 6 m long, found in each **testis** and that links the **seminiferous tubules** to the **vas deferens**. **Sperm** finish maturing in the epididymis.

epigeal germination the germination of a seed in which the **cotyledons** are carried above ground by elongation of a region just below the cotyledons called the hypocotyl.

ethene a plant **growth regulator**, e.g. it speeds up the ripening of some **fruits**.

fertilisation the fusion of a male **gamete** with a female gamete to form the **zygote**.

fetus a human **embryo** once it is recognisably human (after 2–3 months of pregnancy).

follicle a small spherical structure produced by the **ovary** in which an **oocyte** develops. Its development is regulated by hormones from the **pituitary gland**. In fertile humans, one follicle develops per **menstrual cycle**. It later forms the **corpus luteum**.

follicle stimulating hormone (FSH) a hormone secreted by the anterior **pituitary gland**. In females it stimulates development of a **follicle** in the **ovary**. In males it helps to stimulate **sperm** production.

fruit a fertilised **ovary** in a plant. It contains and protects one or more **seeds**. *See also* **parthenocarpy**.

gamete a sex cell that fuses with another gamete during **sexual reproduction**, e.g. **sperm** and **egg**.

gametogenesis the production of **gametes**.

gibberellins a class of plant **growth regulators** that have a number of stimulatory effects, e.g. breaking **dormancy** in cereal seeds, and stimulating stem **growth**, flowering and **fruit** growth in a variety of plants.

gonad an organ which produces **sperm** or **eggs**. The **testes** and **ovaries** are gonads.

gonadotrophin releasing hormone (GnRH) a hormone produced by the **hypothalamus** which stimulates the anterior **pituitary gland** to secrete FSH and LH.

gonadotrophin a class of hormone which stimulate the **gonads** and regulate reproduction, e.g. LH, FSH and **prolactin**.

growth an irreversible increase in dry mass of living material.

growth curve a graph showing **growth**.

growth hormone (GH) a hormone, secreted by the anterior lobe of the **pituitary gland**, that stimulates growth.

growth regulator *or* **plant growth substance** *or* **plant hormone** a chemical found in plants which helps to regulate growth. Five classes are known: **auxins**, **gibberellins**, **cytokinins**, **abscisic acid** and **ethene**.

gynoecium the female reproductive parts of a flower, consisting of one or more **carpels**.

hermaphrodite an organism that produces both male and female **gametes**.

hormone replacement therapy (HRT) the taking of **oestrogen** by women to reduce or prevent the undesirable consequences of **menopause**, e.g. HRT reduces the rate at which osteoporosis develops.

human placental lactogen (HPL) a hormone produced by the **placenta** that stimulates development of the breasts during pregnancy.

hypogeal germination the germination of a seed in which the cotyledons remain in the seed below ground. The first shoot grows from a region just above the cotyledons called the epicotyl.

hypothalamus a part of the forebrain situated above the pituitary gland. It has many functions, including the control of the secretion of hormones by the pituitary gland.

implantation the process of attachment of the **embryo** to the **uterus** wall.

inbreeding sexual reproduction between genetically similar individuals.

inhibin a hormone produced in the male by the Sertoli cells in the **testes**. It helps to regulate **spermatogenesis** by controlling the production of FSH through **negative feedback**.

interstitial cells (*or* **cells of Leydig** *or* **Leydig cells**) cells found between the **seminiferous tubules** in the testes. They make **testosterone**.

interstitial cell stimulating hormone (ICSH) an alternative name for **LH** in the male, where it stimulates the **interstitial cells** in the **testes** to secrete **testosterone**. *See also* **luteinising hormone**.

***in vitro* fertilisation (IVF)** fertilisation outside the body, commonly known as the test tube baby technique. It is used as a treatment for certain causes of infertility and as a means of genetically screening **embryos**.

lactation the production of milk by the breasts. *See also* **prolactin**.

long day plant a plant that flowers in response to long days (short nights).

luteinising hormone (LH) a hormone secreted by the anterior **pituitary gland**. In females it stimulates **ovulation**, release of **progesterone** and the maturing of the ovarian **follicle** into a **corpus luteum**. In males it stimulates secretion of **testosterone**. *See also* **interstitial cell stimulating hormone**.

menopause the cessation of the **menstrual cycle** marking the end of a woman's fertility due to ageing.

menstrual cycle the monthly cycle in the human female during which an **egg** is produced and the **uterus** is prepared for implantation in case of pregnancy.

menstruation the breakdown of the lining of the **uterus** at the end of the **menstrual cycle** if the **egg** is not fertilised.

meristem a region of unspecialised plant cells from which new cells arise by cell division. **Apical meristems** are found at the tips of roots and shoots and cause increases in length. **Lateral meristems** are found along the length of roots and shoots and cause increases in girth.

metamorphosis a change in form from a larva to an adult during an organism's life cycle. **Complete metamorphosis** is a complete change in form, as from caterpillar to butterfly. **Incomplete metamorphosis** is a gradual change in form, as in locusts.

micropropagation the **cloning** of identical cells or small pieces of tissue in an artificial culture to produce genetically identical plants.

monocotyledon a flowering plant which has one **cotyledon** in its **seeds**.

monoecious a plant species which produces separate male and female flowers on the same plant, e.g. oak.

myometrium the muscular outer wall of the **uterus** that contracts during labour and childbirth.

negative feedback a process of self-regulation in which the build-up of a product is responsible for the inhibition of its own production.

oestrogen a hormone secreted by the **ovary**. It stimulates growth of the **uterus**, is involved in **negative feedback** inhibition of FSH and LH, and stimulates breast development during pregnancy.

oocyte sometimes referred to as the **egg**, but strictly the cell from which the egg develops, as follows. The **primary oocyte** is diploid and divides by meiosis I to form a haploid **secondary oocyte** and a polar body. The secondary oocyte divides by meiosis II to form a haploid **egg** and a second polar body.

oogenesis the formation of **eggs**. It takes place in the **ovary**.

oogonium a diploid cell which develops into a primary **oocyte** during **oogenesis**.

outbreeding sexual reproduction between individuals which are not genetically similar.

ovary *In animals:* the organ that produces **eggs** and sex hormones.

    In plants: the swollen base of one or more **carpels**. It contains and protects one or more **ovules**, which become **seeds** after **fertilisation**. The ovary becomes the **fruit** after fertilisation.

oviduct (*or* **fallopian tube**) a tube that leads to the **uterus** from above an **ovary**. It collects the secondary **oocyte** after its release from the **ovary** and is the site of **fertilisation**.

ovulation the release of a secondary **oocyte** from the **ovary**.

ovule one or more structures found in a flower that contain a female **gamete** and become **seeds** after **fertilisation**. *See also* **ovary**.

oxytocin a hormone made in the **hypothalamus** and secreted from the posterior **pituitary gland**. It causes contraction of the **uterus** muscle during labour, and ejaculation of milk from the breasts during breast feeding.

parthenocarpy the ability to produce **fruit** without **pollination**. The fruit is therefore seedless.

photoperiodism the response by an organism to the length of the day. *See also* **long day plant**.

phytochrome a light-sensitive pigment found in plants. It exists in two forms, a red-absorbing form (P_R or P_{660}) and a far-red absorbing form (P_{FR} or P_{730}) and is involved in a range of plant responses to light. *See also* **photoperiodism**.

pituitary gland an endocrine gland attached to the **hypothalamus** of the brain by a short stalk. It secretes a number of different hormones, some of which are concerned with **growth** and **reproduction**, e.g. **GH**, **FSH**, **LH** and **prolactin**. *See also* **gonadotrophin**.

placenta a structure found only in pregnant mammals made partly from tissues of the **embryo** and partly from tissues of the mother. It functions as an organ for exchange of materials between the **embryo** or **fetus** and the mother. It also produces some hormones.

pollen haploid spores produced in the **anthers**. Two male **gametes** develop inside each pollen grain.

pollination the transfer of **pollen** grains from an **anther** to a **stigma**. **Self-pollination** is the transfer of pollen to a stigma on the same flower or to a different flower on the same plant. **Cross-pollination** is the transfer of pollen to a stigma on another plant.

premenstrual tension *or* **syndrome** (**PMT** or **PMS**) the psychological and physical symptoms experienced by some women towards the end of each **menstrual cycle**.

progesterone a hormone secreted by the **ovary**. It stimulates development of the **uterus**, is involved in **negative feedback** inhibition of FSH and LH, and stimulates breast development during pregnancy.

prolactin a hormone secreted by the anterior **pituitary gland** which stimulates the breasts to produce milk.

prolactin releasing factor (**PRF**) a hormone secreted by the **hypothalamus** which stimulates the anterior **pituitary gland** to release **prolactin**.

prostaglandins a group of hormone-like chemicals found in mammals having a wide range of effects, including the contraction of the muscle of the **uterus**.

prostate gland a gland in the male reproductive system that contributes fluid to the **semen**.

protandry the situation when **anthers** mature before **stigmas**. This encourages **cross-pollination**.

protogyny the situation when **stigmas** mature before **anthers**. This encourages **cross-pollination**.

relative growth rate growth rate relative to size, e.g. a baby that grows 2 cm in length has a higher relative growth rate than a teenager who grows 2 cm because the baby was much smaller than the teenager before this growth occurred.

reproduction the production of new organisms by an existing member or members of the same species.

Rhesus factor an antigen found in plasma membranes of the red blood cells of about 84% of humans. Those with the antigen are described as Rhesus positive (RH+), while those without are described as Rhesus negative (RH−).

scarification physical damage to the testa of a **seed** allowing germination.

seed a fertilised **ovule**. It contains and protects an **embryo** and a food store, germinating when conditions are suitable to produce a new plant.

semen fluid containing **sperm** and secretions from the **prostate gland, Cowper's glands** and **seminal vesicles**. It is ejaculated into the vagina of the female during sexual intercourse.

seminal vesicles a pair of glands found in the male reproductive system that contribute **seminal fluid** to the **semen**.

seminiferous tubules tightly coiled tubes, about 1000 of which are found in each **testis**. **Sperm** are made in their walls.

sexual reproduction the fusion of two **gametes** to form a **zygote**.

short day plant a plant that flowers in response to short days (long nights).

sigmoid curve an S-shaped curve. **Absolute growth** curves are often sigmoid in shape.

sperm the male **gamete**.

spermatid an immature **sperm** before its tail develops. *See also* **spermatocyte**.

spermatocyte the cell which develops from a **spermatogonium** and from which **spermatids** develop, as follows. The **primary spermatocyte** is diploid and divides by meiosis I to form two haploid **secondary spermatocytes**. Each of these divides by meiosis II to form two haploid **spermatids**.

spermatogenesis the formation of **sperm**. It takes place in the **testes**.

spermatogonium the diploid cell which develops into a primary **spermatocyte** during **spermatogenesis**.

spermatozoan (*or* **sperm**) the male **gamete**.

stamen the basic unit of the male part of a flower which produces **pollen**. It consists of an **anther** and a filament.

stigma the tip of a **carpel**, which is modified for receiving **pollen**.

style a stalk arising from the **ovary** of a flower which has the **stigma** at its tip.

testa the seed coat, formed after fertilisation from the integuments of the **ovule**. It is usually tough to protect the **seed** and is often involved in the **dormancy** mechanism.

testis the male **gonad**. The site of **spermatogenesis**.

testosterone a hormone made in the **testis** which is needed for the production of **sperm**.

thyroid gland an endocrine organ found in the neck that secretes the hormone **thyroxine**.

thyrotrophin releasing hormone (TRH) a hormone secreted by the **hypothalamus** which stimulates secretion of TSH by the anterior lobe of the **pituitary gland**.

thyroid stimulating hormone (TSH) a hormone secreted by the anterior lobe of the **pituitary gland** which stimulates secretion of **thyroxine** from the **thyroid gland**.

thyroxine a hormone secreted by the **thyroid gland**. It controls basal metabolic rate and stimulates **growth** and **development** in animals.

tissue culture the growth of plant or animal tissues in an artificial culture medium.

urethra the tube that carries urine (and **semen** in the male) to an external opening.

uterus the site where the fertilised **egg** implants and the **placenta** and **fetus** develop. *See also* **myometrium** and **endometrium**.

vas deferens the tube which carries the **sperm** from the **testis** to the **urethra**.

zona pellucida a jelly-like layer surrounding the **oocyte** and secreted by the **follicle** cells.

zygote the diploid cell produced by the fusion of two haploid **gametes** during **sexual reproduction**. It is the first cell of a new organism.

Index

Terms shown in **bold** also appear in the glossary (see pages 107–111). Pages in *italics* refer to figures.